El Teide. Tenerife's, and Spain's, highest mountain. See page 36.

Costa Calma beaches. Great sweeps of white sand draw the visitors to Fuerteventura. See page 84.

La Orotava. A beautifully preserved Tenerife town containing such gems as the Casa de los Balcones. See page 31.

Maspalomas. These pristine dunes on Gran Canaria are like a desert by the sea. See page 63.

Cueva de los Verdes. Impressive lava formations on Lanzarote. See page 77.

El Hierro ... ee page 41.

D0318473

A PERFECT DAY

9.00am Breakfast

Soak up the sea views at Playa de las Vistas and breakfast at the Water Melon (Centro Comercial San Telmo) in San Telmo, Los Cristianos.

11.30am Arguayo

Rejoin the main road going north. After Chio head right via the village of Arguayo, home to the Museum of 'Cha Domitila' (tel: 922 863 465), where you can watch potters at work and purchase ceramics.

12.30pm Masca

Carry on north via Las Manchas to Santiago del Teide. From here continue to Tenerife's most picturesque village – Masca, at the head of a dramatic gorge. Enjoy the breathtaking views from one of the roadside restaurants – Chez Arlette, El Guanche (Calle El Lomito 9, tel: 922 863 027) is a good bet.

10.00am Adeje

Take the main TF1 road north and divert to the unspoilt hill town of Adeje, former seat of the Guanche tribe and later stronghold of the Counts of Gomera. Visit the remains of their Casa Fuerte and amble along the steep Rambla with its bars and cafés. Adeje is the entry point to the Barranca del Infierno (Hell's Gorge), a popular 4-mile (6.3km) return hike which should be saved for another day.

IN TENERIFE

4.00pm **West Coast**

Head back south on the main road, then at Tamaimo turn on to the TF454 down the valley for Los Gigantes. 'The Giants' is named after the soaring volcanic walls that drop sheer into the sea. Continue south along the coast, pausing perhaps at the fishing village-cum-beach resort of Playa de San Juan.

11.00pm **Nightlife**

End the evening at the über-cool El Faro Chill Art (CC Torviscas Playa, tel: 922 712 842) between Puerto Colón and Fañabe Beach, watching the sun sink from the Zen terrace – before partying at the disco inside.

2.00pm **Garachico**

Return to the main road and head north (TF82) for the charming coastal village of Garachico. Spend a couple of hours here, taking a dip in the lava rock pools, visiting the ex-Convent of San Francisco, admiring the views from Castillo de San Miguel or cooling off with a drink in the Plaza.

7.00pm **Sunset Wining and Dining**

Enjoy a cocktail at La Caleta on the Costa Adeje, then tuck into superb seafood gourmet food at Restaurant 88, Masía del Mar (tel: 922 775 829; www.restaurant88tenerife.com; tel: 922 710 895) or Piscis Terraza (tel: 922 710 241), with stunning views over the Atlantic Ocean.

CONTENTS

INTRODUCTION

More than 1,000km (620 miles) south of the Iberian Peninsula and just 115km (70 miles) from the nearest point on the African coast, an archipelago made up of 13 volcanic islands juts dramatically out of the Atlantic Ocean. These, the Canary Islands, are an integral part of Spain, although they now have their own island government, known as the Cabildo Insular. Six of the islands, Alegranza, La Graciosa, Lobos, Montaña Clara, Roque del Este and Roque del Oeste, are no more than specks in the sea and remain uninhabited. Of the others, it is the eastern islands, the three closest to Africa – Gran Canaria, Lanzarote and Fuerteventura – that are geologically the oldest, and as they have the most extensive coastal shelf, they also have the most beaches.

The four western islands, Tenerife, La Palma, La Gomera and El Hierro, in descending order of size, have ragged coastlines with cliffs rising vertiginously out of the ocean. Of these, however, only Tenerife has beaches of any size, and the golden sands that make them so popular have usually been imported from the Sahara or rescued from the bottom of the sea. In total, the archipelago has approximately 1,500km (930 miles) of coast and the characteristic, intensely blue waters are due to the ocean's depth – as much as 3,000m (9,840ft) between some of the islands.

What's in a name?

The Canary Islands are believed to have been named after the dogs seen there during Roman times – *canis* being Latin for dog. Their Spanish descendants, the popular *Presa Canario* (Canarian dog of prey), are similar to mastiffs.

Charco Manso arch, El Hierro

Climate, Flora and Fauna

Geographically within the bounds of the Tropic of Cancer, the surrounding ocean is somewhat cooler than would be expected at such a sub-tropical latitude. The Gulf current arrives from the north and the ensuing trade winds that brush the islands brings the Canaries, at sea level at least, an extremely genial climate. Average temperatures on the beaches vary around 19°C (66°F) in winter and 25°C (77°F) in summer. However, many of the islands are mountainous – Mount Teide on Tenerife rises to 3,718m (12,195ft) and not only dominates the archipelago but is the highest mountain in Spain. Such altitudes mean that the temperatures can vary dramatically, not only between islands, but within islands as well.

Prickly pear on Gran Canaria

The combination of such a climate and the unusual geological features have given rise to an amazing array of flora and fauna, which thrives even though none of the islands has a running river. The isolation of the archipelago has also played its part in the preservation of these natural gifts. In fact, with around 650 native plant species, it is one of the most important areas in the world, comparable only with other archipelagos such as Hawaii and the Galapagos. Recognising this, and intent upon preserving it, the Law of Natural Areas in the Canaries has created nature and rural parks, nature reserves, nature monuments, protected landscapes and areas of scientific interest, with the intention of limiting human activity in the zones. These amount to no less than 36 percent of the archipelago's territory.

Aloe

The climate of the Canary Islands is ideal for the growth of aloe, widely thought to alleviate skin conditions and now used in moisturisers, soaps, sunscreens and shampoos. Christopher Columbus is said to have remarked during a voyage that 'there are four essential things that a man needs to feel good: wheat, grapes, olives and aloe.'

People and Tourism

Governed by the Spanish since the end of the 15th century the Canarians, to outsiders, look Spanish, speak Spanish, are imbued with Spanish culture and to all intents and purposes are little different – except perhaps that they are somewhat quieter and less volatile in character than their mainland cousins. However, throughout the centuries the Canary Islands have acted as a bridge between Europe, Africa and the Americas and as a consequence have become home to numerous people originating from disparate cultures, especially from the Latin American countries that were once Spanish colonies. The result, today, is a people who regard themselves as Canarian first and Spanish second.

The islanders learned, in the second half of the 20th century, to capitalise on their natural resources – the fine climate and splendid beaches that attract so many visitors from northern Europe. Tourism is a massive business. In 2014 the islands were visited by nearly 12 million people, with the majority (around 9 million) heading for Tenerife and Gran Canaria and just over 1 million each to Lanzarote and Fuerteventura. Certain areas, mainly the southern coasts of Gran Canaria and Tenerife, and to a lesser but growing extent Lanzarote and Fuerteventura, cater to mass tourism, while the smaller islands, that lack commercially exploitable beaches, will always lag well behind in numbers, if not in their natural attractions. It would seem that with so many visitors, the islands would be perpetually crowded, but this is not so, as most people head directly for the major resorts, such as Playa de las Américas in Tenerife and Playa del Inglés in Gran Canaria. In fact, if all the land devoted to tourism were to be added up, it would still occupy only a mere fraction of the islands' total area and natural wealth.

Which is the Best Island for You?

It may be a cliché, but it is nonetheless true, that there is something for everyone. The diversity of landscapes on the islands is quite amazing. Snow-capped mountains, beautiful, verdant valleys, deserts, towering cliffs and wonderful beaches of golden or black sand can all be found in the Canaries and some islands have intriguing combinations of these characteristics. Remember, the Canaries are volcanic, and volcanic islands are never dull. Teneguia, on La Palma, erupted as recently as 1971. In Lanzarote you can not only gaze at the awesome scenery created by earth-shattering events that occurred centuries ago, you can also watch your lunch cooking over the heat of the volcano beneath your feet (see page 72).

Tenerife is the biggest island and has plenty to show for it. Mount Teide offers the grandest scenery and the island certainly has the greatest number of tourist attractions by day and night. In terms of all-round appeal, however, Gran Canaria runs a close second. Both islands have bustling modern cities and sleepy old towns to visit; both have dramatic and strikingly beautiful interiors; and both have busy resorts ranging from raucous to tranquil.

Playa de las Cucharas on Lanzarote's Costa Teguise

If a long stretch of golden beach is a priority, then southern Gran Canaria has the edge. Lanzarote, with its stark *malpaís* (badlands), will delight those who are environmentally aware yet enjoy the company of other visitors. Whether or not the continued growth of tourism there erodes this delicate balance remains to be seen, but the tourist attractions masterminded by local artist César Manrique (1919–92) combine well with those of resorts like Puerto del Carmen, and the general ambience of this island, with its low-rise, whitewashed buildings is extremely appealing.

Fuerteventura tends to polarise opinion: it is truly a desert island – wind-swept, sandy and barren. The beaches here are certainly the best in the Canaries and resorts to suit most tastes are springing up. Aside from water sports, for which it has a high reputation, there isn't a great deal to do or see. The lesser known and much smaller islands of La Palma, La Gomera and El Hierro do not have that many beaches and have therefore escaped mass

Festival fun, El Hierro

tourism and should continue to do so, although they are cultivating low-key *turismo rural*. The lack of commercial attractions this brings has, for these three islands, become an attraction in itself.

There are relatively few hotels and restaurants of note (although enough for discerning visitors), no discos and blaring bars to disturb the peace and very few tourists. There is a bountiful supply of beautiful mountainous scenery and, if you search hard enough, a pleasant beach or two to relax on. If this is your idea of a dream holiday, one of these quieter islands may be perfect for you.

For most people, though, a day or two away from it all is enough. Island hopping is easy and a few days on an unspoiled island combined with the creature comforts of a major resort can offer the best of both worlds. Travel independently, look out for the unexpected, and you will soon discover that the Canary Islands have much more to offer than just an all-year-round suntan.

A BRIEF HISTORY

The Canary Islands are a place of myths and legends. Many writers link the lost continent of Atlantis with the Canaries. According to Plato this rich, happy land, somewhere west of Gibraltar in the Atlantic Ocean, was destroyed by earthquakes and tidal waves nearly 12,000 years ago. After the cataclysm only the mountain tops of Atlantis remained above the sea and constituted seven islands. Could this have been the Canaries? The ancient Greeks thought of the islands as the Garden of Hesperides, and the Romans called this archipelago the 'Insulae Fortunatae', the Fortunate Islands.

The author Plutarch wrote of fertile lands somewhere off the coast of Africa, where the breezes of springtime never stop. His source was the Roman leader Sertorius, who had heard of the lands from an explorer. In the 1st century AD Pliny wrote of an expedition to the islands by King Jube II of Mauretania, who apparently saw many dogs roaming the islands. *Canis* is the Latin for dogs, hence Canary Islands.

The First Inhabitants

Long before the first European sailors arrived, all seven of the main Canary Islands were inhabited. The original people are known as Guanches, meaning 'man' in the native tongue. Strictly speaking, this name applies only to the inhabitants of Tenerife, but has come to be widely used for the indigenous people of the whole archipelago.

End of the world

In the 2nd century AD, when there was no doubt in the minds of mankind that the world was flat, El Hierro, the westernmost of the Canary Islands, became the official western edge of the world. This was because the mathematician and astronomer Ptolemy (AD150) based his prime meridian here, and it was commonly used until the 19th century.

The Guanches are thought to have arrived on the islands around the 1st or 2nd century BC, probably from North Africa. Ethnographers link them with the Cro-Magnon and Proto-Mediterranean race. They were tall, light-skinned, often blue-eyed and fair-haired. You can see their remains in the meticulous collection of the Museo Canario in Las Palmas on Gran Canaria (see page 61). Here too you can study their preoccupation with death. Like the ancient Egyptians, they carefully embalmed their dead, presumably for a ceremonial passage to the next world. Cryptic rock carvings have been found that may explain these rituals, but so far no one has found the Canarian version of the Rosetta Stone with which to decipher them.

The Guanches were cave dwellers, although many of the caves that remain today were probably used only for storage. The Cenobio de Valerón near Gáldar in Gran Canaria, for example, although called a convent, was probably only a grain store (see page 66). Cave dwelling in such a climate is a logical idea, being cooler in summer and warmer in winter than more conventional accommodation. Even today, there are many cave dwellings on the islands.

A Guanche legacy that you will see at the market place and in traditional eating houses is *gofio*, a finely-ground, toasted flour that is still a traditional Canarian staple. The Guanche language also lives on in such place names as Tafira and Tamadaba (in Gran Canaria), Timanfaya (in Lanzarote), Teide (in Tenerife) and Tenerife itself.

Maritime mystery

How the Guanches came to arrive on the islands is a mystery as no evidence of any boats has ever been discovered. One theory is that they may have floated across from North Africa on craft made of reeds. The expeditions of Thor Heyerdahl lend some credence to this idea and the concept is explored in great detail at the Pyramids of Güimar in Tenerife (see page 39).

Conquistadors

The first foreign visitors to the Canaries are thought to have been Arab sailors who landed on Gran Canaria some 2,000 years ago and were given a warm welcome. In later centuries, the islanders' gracious hospitality was to cost them dearly.

Guanche chief

Europeans did not arrive until the 14th century, when the Genoese sailor Lanzarotto Marcello colonised the island that was known then as Tytheroygatra and subsequently as Lanzarote. Slave traders, treasure seekers and missionaries all followed in Lanzarotto's wake, but it was not until 1402 that the European conquest of the Canaries began in earnest. At its helm was the Norman baron, Jean de Béthencourt, in the service of Henry III of Castile. After the baron had taken Lanzarote and Fuerteventura with comparative ease, his ships were scattered by storms off Gran Canaria. He next turned to El Hierro, where the awestruck islanders welcomed as gods the new visitors arriving in their great floating vessels. Béthencourt returned the hospitality by inviting them onto his ships. He then took them captive and sold them into slavery.

Around this time the Portuguese, who had also been colonising the Atlantic, turned their attention to the Canaries. Naval skirmishes ensued between the two powers, but at

Jean de Béthancourt

the end of the war of succession between Portugal and Castile, the wide-ranging Treaty of Alcaçovas ended Lisbon's claims to the Fortunate Islands. By order of Ferdinand and Isabella of Castile, the second phase of the conquest was set in motion. By 1483 Gran Canaria had been subdued, followed by La Gomera in 1488. La Palma held out until 1493 and after another two years of furious fighting, the biggest prize of all, Tenerife, was in Spanish hands. The process of pacification and conversion to the Christian faith had taken almost a century of bloody guerilla warfare with thousands of casualties, the majority being the brave but ill-equipped Guanches.

Columbus Connections

Just as the conquest of the Canaries was reaching its climax, Christopher Columbus (Cristóbal Colón in Spanish) was planning his expedition in search of a sea route to the East Indies. Each of the Canaries claims some connection with Columbus, who came to the islands because they were then the world's most westerly charted points and therefore the last stopping point before venturing into the unknown.

The great navigator stopped off at La Gomera and at Las Palmas (for ship repairs) on his voyage of 1492 and he recorded a volcanic eruption while passing Tenerife. His crew took this as an ill omen but, as history tells us, once past El Hierro they did not drop off the edge of the world after all. Columbus's routes and Canarian connections may be traced at the atmospheric Casa de Colón in Las Palmas (see page 60).

Wine and Warfare

The Canaries' first major agricultural enterprise was sugar. Sugar cane sprouted easily on the islands and, during the first half of the 16th century, a burgeoning industry developed. Boom turned to bust, however, with cheaper sugar production from Brazil and the Antilles, and the industry died.

Still, trade links had at least been established with both the Old and the New Worlds, and wine became the new venture to bolster the economy, especially in Tenerife. Grapes grown in the volcanic soil produced a distinctive, full-bodied malmsey wine (*malvasía*) that became the fashionable drink of aristocratic Europe. Shakespeare and Voltaire, among others, were lavish in their praise and today's island visitors can still sample the excellent wine in *bodegas*, restaurants, or even from the *supermercado*. When touring the islands you may still see old disused wine presses (*lagares*) on hillsides.

By the end of the 18th century the Canaries were a sufficiently important trading point to attract all types of incursions. In 1797, Admiral Horatio Nelson attacked Santa Cruz de Tenerife in search of a Spanish treasure ship. The defenders responded vigorously, accounting for the lives of 226 British sailors and the removal of the lower part of Nelson's saluting arm. The Santa Cruzeros clearly had no hard feelings towards Admiral Nelson, however. Once it was known that the attack had been repelled, a gift of wine was sent out to his ship. Nelson returned the compliment by sending the governor cheese and a cask of beer. The captured British flags are stored in a glass case in Nuestra Señora de la Concepción.

San Cristóbal de la Laguna,
the island's first capital

Free Trade

By the early 19th century, Canarians had become fully Spanish in both outlook and loyalties and many volunteers fought in the Peninsular War (Spaniards call it the War of Independence), which ended in 1814 with the restoration of Ferdinand VII to the Spanish throne.

Economic problems arose in the early 19th century and the wine industry started to fail. Luckily, another single-crop opportunity presented itself in the form of cochineal, a parasitic beetle attracted to the *opuntia* variety of cactus. The tiny bodies of the female bugs contain a dark-red liquid perfect for dyeing and for 50 years or so, millions of bugs were crushed for the sake of the Canarian economic good.

The bubble burst with the rise of chemical dyes in the 1870s. With the failure of yet another monoculture, the Spanish government felt constrained to help the Canarian economy. In the mid-19th century, free-port status was granted by royal decree to one port on each of the islands (two in Tenerife). The lowering of duties and trade barriers at a time of considerable shipping expansion had the desired effect and Santa Cruz de Tenerife and Las Palmas soon became two of the world's busiest ports. British entrepreneurs also invested a lot of money in the port of Las Palmas.

The most recent monoculture was bananas. The first exports were made in the 1880s, but the trade's runaway success did not outlast World War I. However, the cultivation of the small, sweet bananas continued to be a mainstay of the islands' economy for as long as mainland Spain was able to provide a guaranteed market.

In 1912, Cabildos (Island Councils) were created and given the responsibility for the social, political and economic administration of each island and coordination with the Ayuntamientos (Town Halls). This led, in 1927, to the Canaries being divided into two provinces; Santa Cruz de Tenerife with the western islands of Tenerife, La Palma, La Gomera and El Hierro; and Las Palmas de Gran Canaria with the eastern islands of Lanzarote and Fuerteventura.

The Spanish Civil War

The plot that sparked off the Spanish Civil War was hatched in the Canary Islands. In 1936, a group of senior officers, discontented with the policies of the Spanish Republican Government, met in secret in the woods of La Esperanza in Tenerife. They had come to meet a fellow officer, Francisco Franco, a right-wing nationalist whom the government had packed off to the Canaries as governor in the hope that he would do less damage there. From the Canaries, Franco took off for North Africa, the launching pad for the insurgent right-wing attack. Three years later his armies had

Bridge to the New World

The role of the islands as a bridge between the Old World and the New has continued through the centuries. Canarians have settled in Latin America in large numbers, usually in search of a better way of life, and news from Venezuela and Cuba is treated almost as a local item in the Canary Islands' newspapers. Canarian bananas provided the stock for those of the Caribbean and, in accent and musical rhythms, the speech of the Canaries lies halfway between Spain and South America.

triumphed in a ruthless struggle that cost around a million Spanish lives.

The Canaries were not spared the horrors of the war (mass Republican executions took place in the aptly named Barranco del Infierno, the Gorge of Hell, in Tenerife), but on the whole the islands prospered during Franco's dictatorship (which lasted until his death in 1975).

Tourism and Environment

The massive growth of tourism on the islands since the 1960s has, in some cases, literally refaced the landscape, with brand new resorts such as Playa de las Américas in Tenerife and Playa del Inglés in Gran Canaria, springing up like Gold Rush boom towns. However, such developments, although they have given the Canaries their current mass-tourism image, are the exception. Whole swathes of the more developed islands are still virtually untouched, while La Palma, La Gomera and El Hierro have only in recent years started to provide tourist facilities. The infrastructure and transport systems both within and between the islands have, as a consequence, improved enormously.

Following the death of Franco, a constitutional monarchy was restored under Juan Carlos I. However, the subsequent decolonisation of Spain's Western Saharan possessions resulted in a movement of many thousands of people back to the Canary Islands, creating social and logistical problems.

The declaration of a new Spanish Constitution in 1978 further strengthened the new democracy and prepared the way for a Statute of Autonomous Regions. In 1982, the Canary Islands were given autonomous status, with many governmental functions transferred from Madrid to the Cabildo Insular, and the status of capital shared between Santa Cruz de Tenerife and Las Palmas de Gran Canaria. Each island has its own local Cabildo or Council and officials are elected by free vote every four years. In 1986, Spain became part of the EEC (now European Union); this brought the end of the Canary Islands' duty-free port status, but certain special allowances were negotiated. The islands were fully integrated into the EU in 1995.

Despite the economic benefits that tourism has brought, local authorities became aware of the dangers of unchecked development and an unpleasant 'lager lout' image. As a result, there has been an emphasis on a new image for the tourist industry. Ancient paths (*caminos rurales*) have been opened up for hiking in the central peaks of Gran Canaria and the northeast of Tenerife, and EU funds have helped promote *turismo rural*, creating country hotels and helping convert traditional buildings into holiday accommodation. All this is part of a drive to encourage conservation-conscious tourism and attract

Agriculture is still an important part of the economy

Tourism, the new monoculture

people with a love of the countryside.

When mainland Spain tightened its immigration restrictions in 2005, a new type of visitor began arriving on the Canaries: illegal immigrants from sub-Saharan Africa. An estimated 25,000 made the perilous journey in 2006, and many more drowned or died of dehydration along the way. Other headlines have included the forest fires that ravaged Tenerife and Gran Canaria in 2007; strong winds, high temperatures and low humidity allowed the blaze to spread across 24,000 hectares of land, forcing the evacuation of more than 11,000 people. The islands were ravaged by fire again in 2012, when about 25 percent of the Garajonay nature reserve, a Unesco World Heritage site on La Gomera Island, was burnt down. In the same year the Spanish Supreme Court rejected appeals from environmental organisations and gave the green light for the Repsol oil company to start offshore oil explorations. This drew an angry response from the islanders as three out of four Canarians opposed the drilling.

Images of these events perhaps helped to add another dimension to people's perception of these islands, as more than just a playground for northern Europeans in search of fun, sun and sand.

Historical Landmarks

circa **3000BC** Settlers arrive from North Africa.

AD1339 Genoese Lanzarotto Malocello discovers Lanzarote.

1402–6 Norman Jean de Béthencourt conquers Lanzarote, Fuerteventura and El Hierro for Spain.

15th century The Guanches resist the Spanish invaders until Tenerife, the last island, is brought under control of the Spanish Crown in1495.

1492 Columbus briefly stops at Las Palmas before sailing to America.

circa **1500** Sugar cane introduced and African slaves imported. From 1554, the sugar industry starts to decline.

16th–17th centuries Many inhabitants of impoverished Lanzarote and Fuerteventura turn to piracy. Wine production replaces sugar.

1730–6 Continuous eruptions of Mount Timanfaya in Lanzarote.

1700–1950 Poverty forces widespread emigration to Latin America.

1825–75 A short economic boom follows the introduction of the cochineal beetle. Prosperity ended by invention of chemical dyes.

1852 Isabella II declares the Canary Islands a Free Trade Zone.

1890 The British introduce bananas as a monoculture.

1936 Franco, military governor of the Canary Islands, initiates the three-year Spanish Civil War.

1956 The first charter plane lands on Gran Canaria, followed by direct flights to Tenerife in 1959, and tourism takes off.

1978–82 Spain forms the Autonomous Region of the Canary Islands.

1986 Spain joins the EU and negotiates a special status for the Canaries.

1995 Islands integrated into the EU but retain important tax privileges.

1971 Teneguia, on La Palma, erupts.

2002 The euro becomes the national currency.

2006 Sharp rise in the number of illegal immigrants from Africa.

2007 Summer fires devastate the Mogán region of Gran Canaria.

2012 Repsol begins offshore oil explorations amid widespread protests. Fires ravage Garajonay nature reserve on La Gomera.

2015 General elections in Spain.

WHERE TO GO

TENERIFE

Tenerife is the largest of the Canaries, with an area of some 2,045 sq km (790 sq miles) and a population of nearly 900,000. It offers the visitor more sights, more attractions, more towns and cities to explore and more contrasts than any of the other islands, from banana plantations to sandy beaches and snow-capped mountains. Tenerife has been welcoming visitors from cold northern climes since the 19th century. However, the focus has changed from the cloudy, green north coast where Puerto de la Cruz was once the favourite resort (it is still enormously popular), to the hot, arid south.

Santa Cruz de Tenerife

In the northeast of the island, **Santa Cruz**, the capital of Tenerife, the principal port and the administrative centre for the westerly Canaries, is not a city in which visitors spend a great deal of time. However, there are some pleasant parks and squares, a lively shopping and eating area and a number of interesting museums and churches. The main square, **Plaza de España**, has undergone a complete transformation by architects Jacques Herzog and Pierre de Mueron, who also renovated the Tate Modern gallery in London. The new focal point of the square is an open space around a circular pool of salt water with a geyser, while the rest of the area is filled with trees. The **Monumento de los Caídos**, dedicated to the fallen Nationalists in the Civil War, has been integrated into the new design.

The Art Deco building beside it, with a clock tower, is the **Cabildo Insular** (island government headquarters), and the

Dramatic landscape in the Parque Nacional del Teide

Playa de las Teresitas, Tenerife

tourist office is next door. The **Calle del Castillo**, the principal shopping street, heads inland from the square. Off to the right is the **Museo Municipal de Bellas Artes** (open Tues–Fri 10am–8pm, Sat–Sun 10am–3pm; free) which has some impressive pictures. Further north, up Calle San Francisco, is the **Museo Militar** (open Tues–Sat 10am–2pm; free) which houses El Tigre, the cannon from which the shot that shattered Admiral Nelson's arm in 1797 was allegedly fired.

Beside the Barranco de Santos, stands the **Iglesia de Nuestra Señora de la Concepción** (Church of the Immaculate Conception), dating from the early 16th century. The streets around the church, particularly Calle Dominguez Alfonso, come alive in the evenings, with busy bars and *tascas* (pubs) open until the early hours. On the other side of the *barranco* (a dry river bed) is the **Museo de la Naturaleza y el Hombre** (open Tues–Sat 9am–8pm, Sun–Mon 10am–5pm; www.museosdetenerife.org), with exhibits illustrating the lives and the death rituals of Guanche society; and the **Mercado de Nuestro Señora de Àfrica**, commonly known as La Recova (www.la-recova.com), a colourful fruit, flower and vegetable market.

Near the port stands the elegant **Auditorio** de Tenerife Adán Martín (guided tours Mon–Sat at 12.30pm, www.

auditoriodetenerife.com), a concert hall designed by Basque architect Santiago Calatrava, which is home to the Tenerife Symphony Orchestra. Beside it is a bus station and behind it, beyond the old **Castillo San Juan**, is the **Parque Marítimo César Manrique** (open daily 10am–6pm), an area of seawater pools, with trees, flowers and waterfalls.

North of the city lies the **Playa de las Teresitas**, the city beach, a long stretch of golden sand, imported from the Sahara in the 1970s, which is busy with locals at the weekends. The nearby town of San Andrés has a good seafood restaurant (see page 110).

Puerto de la Cruz

Puerto de la Cruz has been attracting northern Europeans for more than a century and it maintains much of its colonial grandeur. The seafront promenade has been quite heavily commercialised but not spoiled, and the atmosphere is always lively without being boisterous. The main square, the **Plaza del Charco de los Camarones** (Square of the Shrimp Pool), is the hub of both tourist and local life, and the cafés, restaurants and shops are busy at all hours.

Just off the square, the old town around the **Puerto Pesquero** is remarkably oblivious to change. Among the narrow streets, with faded wooden balconies and carved doors, are the 18th-century **Casa de Miranda**, which houses a *bodeguita* and fish restaurant, and, facing the tiny port, the **Casa de la Real Aduana** (Customs House), the oldest building in town, dating from 1620. On the top floor is the **Museo de Arte Contemporáneo Eduardo Westerdahl** (MACEW, Museum of Contemporary Art, Mon–Thur and Sat 10am–2pm, Fri also 5–7.30pm) with an interesting collection and the main cultural centre in town.

Nearby (going west) you will come to the Hotel Monopol (www.monopoltf.com) one of Puerto's oldest, with beautiful balconies; and, in the Plaza de la Iglesia, the town's principal

Puerto de la Cruz' built-up waterfront

church, **Iglesia de Nuestra Señora de la Penna de Francia**, built in 1697.

The problem of lack of a decent beach in Puerto was brilliantly addressed by the late Lanzarote artist César Manrique. He designed **Lago Martiánez** (open daily 10am–7pm, winter 10am–6pm), a 3-hectare (8-acre) complex of tropical lagoons, cascading fountains and sunbathing terraces, cleverly landscaped with lush palms, sculptures and black-and-white volcanic rocks to fit perfectly into the seafront, where the surf crashes spectacularly against the rocks. The Lago is also known as the Lido San Telmo after the gleaming white Iglesia de San Telmo, dedicated to sailors, nearby.

Just to the west of Puerto is **Loro Parque** (open daily 8.30am–6.45pm; www.loroparque.com), with what may be the world's largest collection of parrots – more than 300 species. It is home to an eclectic array of creatures, including chimpanzees, gorillas, alligators and sea-lions. There is also an aquarium and shark tunnel, a splendid dolphinarium, and Planet Penguin, a natural habitat for the penguins.

Just north of Puerto, on the road to La Orotavo, there is the **Jardín de Aclimatación de la Orotava** or **Jardín Botánico** (Botanical Garden; open daily 9am–6pm), founded by royal decree in 1788. Covering some 2.5 hectares (6 acres) – and being extended by another 2 hectares – it has palms of every variety and the centrepiece is a huge South American fig tree whose enormous branches and roots have become intertwined into one great tree house.

La Orotava

La Orotava is a remarkably well-preserved, unspoiled old town set on a steep hill above Puerto de la Cruz. Stately mansions, ancient churches and cobbled streets are its trademarks. The twin towers, baroque façade and Byzantine dome of the **Iglesia de Nuestra Señora de la Concepción** (rebuilt after earthquake damage in 1705) dominate a skyline that has changed little for centuries. Continue up Calle San Francisco to the splendid, 17th-century **Casa de los Balcones** (open Mon–Sat 8.30am–7.30pm, Sun 8.30am–1.30pm; admission fee for museum only; www.casa-balcones.com). The balconies are in the courtyard and are some of the finest of their kind. The house has long been associated with

Painting with Sand

To celebrate the feast of Corpus Christi, around the end of May or in June, detailed and quite extraordinary works of art are made by spreading multi-coloured volcanic rock and sand particles on the ground in the same way that a conventional artist would spread paint onto a canvas. The plaza in front of the Palacio Municipal in La Orotava is the site for the most acclaimed piece of artwork. Similar pictures are created with flowers and leaves in La Laguna and a few other towns. (See page 96.)

Preparing the floral display for the Corpus Christi procession

lace-making, and assistants in traditional costume will show you what's on offer, and hope that you will buy.

The **Casa del Turista**, opposite, is almost as grand, and is part of the same outlet for island wares and lace. Also worth visiting is the **Museo de Cerámica** (open Mon–Sat 10am–6pm, Sun 10am–4pm) in Casa Tafuriaste, a studio with a collection of traditional Spanish ceramics.

Going North

El Sauzal is important for its wines. Signs lead to the **Casa del Vino La Baranda** (open Wed–Sat 9am–9pm, Sun 11am–6pm, Tues 11.30am–6.30pm; free; www.casadel vinotenerife.com). You can see how the wine is made, then enjoy tastings and make purchases from the shop. There is a bar and restaurant, with fine views over the coast. **Tacoronte**, nearby, is renowned for a venerated 17th-century figure of Christ, **Cristo de los Dolores y Agonía** (Christ of Sorrows and Agony), in the monastery church in the Plaza del Cristo.

San Cristóbal de La Laguna

San Cristóbal de La Laguna, declared a Unesco World Heritage Site in 1999, is Tenerife's second-largest town, known as the cultural capital of the island; there has been a university here since 1701. Start at the **Plaza del Adelantado**, where the neoclassical **Ayuntamiento** (Town Hall) and the baroque **Palacio de Nava** are two secular highlights. In between is the massive **Iglesia-Convento de Santa Catalina de Siena**, with an ornate Canarian balcony. A short way along Calle Obispo Rey Redondo is the **Cathedral** (Santa Iglesia Catedral de San Cristóbal de La Laguna), with twin bell towers. The original, 16th-century building fell into disrepair, and this one dates from 1904. Further along is the town's oldest church, the **Iglesia de Nuestra Señora de la Concepción**, built in 1502. Its seven-storey belfry and watchtower were added two centuries later. The interior is outstanding, with exquisite timber carvings on the ceiling, pulpit and choir stalls. The font was used to baptise converted Guanche leaders.

You can see the interior of an historic mansion in Calle San Agustin, where Casa Lercaro houses the **Museo de Historia y Archivo Insular** (open Tue–Sat 9am–8pm, Sun–Mon 10am– 5pm; Fri–Sat 4–8pm free; www.museodetenerife.org).

West of Puerto

A day's outing from Puerto de la Cruz along the north and west coasts covers some of the island's most spectacular scenery. Sleepy Icod de Los Vinos is famous as the home of the botanical freak that is **Drago Milenario**, a huge dragon tree estimated to be 800 years old.

Drago Milenario

Continue west on the coast road from Icod to **Garachico** and after 6km (3.5miles) the tortuous descent begins. There are marvellous views down onto this compact little town, set on a small peninsula with waves crashing all around. The peninsula was formed from the volcanic debris deposited by an eruption in 1709, when most of the town and its inhabitants were destroyed. The best viewpoint is the **Mirador de Garachico**.

A lucky survivor nearby is the beautifully preserved, 16th-century **Castillo de San Miguel** (www.castillosanmiguel. com), which provides an atmospheric setting for evenings of medieval entertainment. There is no beach, but a cleverly designed set of pools built into the rocks more than compensates. Garachico is a little gem: neat houses with attractive balconies line cobbled streets and old churches adorn pretty squares. The main square, Plaza de la Libertad is shady and attractive and is dominated by the **Iglesia de Nuestra Señora de Los Angeles**, and the 16th-century convent of Francis of Assisi, which now holds the art space **Casa de Piedra**. A museum of contemporary art is housed in the 17th-century former convent of Santo Domingo.

About 8km (5 miles) along the coast road, past Buenavista del Norte, lies the most westerly point in Tenerife, the **Punta de Teno** with its lighthouse (1896). From here there are panoramic views across to La Gomera and south to the massive cliffs of Los Gigantes. Turn back to Buenavista and take a marked turn inland to Masca. Be warned, though, that this is not a drive

An Ancient, Mystical Tree

The dragon tree *(Draecana draco)*, which dates from the prehistoric tertiary period, is unique to the Canary Islands. It held a mystical quality for the Guanches, who saw it as a symbol of fertility and wisdom, using its bark on their shields when they went to war. Its resin, known as dragon's blood, turns red on contact with the air, and was used to embalm the Guanche dead. In Europe other uses were found for it; to dye hair golden, to stain marble red and to varnish violins.

to be undertaken by inexperienced or nervous drivers.

Initially the road, climbing up the arable hillsides, is no easy to negotiate, but this soon changes once the entrance to the vertiginous valley is reached. Until the first road was built in 1972, the picturesque village of **Masca** could only be reached on the back of a donkey. All around is some of the most dramatic scenery on the island, but if you are driving, you won't have any time to savour it. The road clings precariously to the side of lush, green mountains cleft by deep, dark ravines and often zig-zags on itself in the

The infamous road to Masca

tightest of hairpin bends. It is not unknown to have to reverse back down and around these bends, allowing other vehicles to pass. At Masca, relax at one of the restaurants and enjoy the stupendous scenery before continuing south on an equally difficult drive, to re-join the main road at Santiago del Teide. The area was badly affected by the fires of July 2007, and Masca was evacuated. The tiny village is now back on its feet, but still needs a lot of improvements.

A little further south, turn off towards the resort of **Puerto de Santiago** (which has a good beach) then walk out to the edge of the marina jetty to get the best view of the enormous sheer cliffs, up to 800m (2,625ft) high, which are appropriately known as **Los Gigantes** (The Giants). A small port of the same name has developed into a busy resort. It is a popular diving centre and, although there is only a small, black sand beach, you can swim in an artificial seawater lido.

The Central Area

There are four main roads up to the **Parque Nacional del Teide**, (www.parquesnacionalesdecanarias.es) so it is always accessible, wherever you are on the island. The most picturesque route is via **La Esperanza**. The small town soon gives way to a lush forest of giant pines and eucalyptus trees, the Bosque de La Esperanza. Four km (2.5 miles) south at **Las Raíces** is where Franco met with his co-conspirators in 1936 (see page 21). An obelisk commemorates the event. As the road gains altitude and temperatures fall, the views become ever more spectacular. The gleaming white towers you see off to the east belong to the **Observatorio Astronómico del Teide** (guided tours by appointment only, book at www. volcanolife.com; tel: 922 329 110; www.iac.es) where, due to the excellent astronomic quality of the skies, priority is being given to studying the sun.

The entrance to the National Park is **El Portillo**, where a Visitor Centre (open daily 9am–4.15pm) has information about daily signposted and guided walks, and a 4-hectare (10-acre) garden growing and breeding native, high altitude plants. A road running through the park is dotted with *miradors* (viewing points) offering spectacular views. Unless you are up for a five-hour climb, the last part of the journey to the summit (Pico del Teide) has to be made by **Teleférico** (cable car), 8km (5 miles) south of the Visitor Centre, and close to the **Parador Nacional del Teide** (www.parador.es), the only accommodation in

Moonscape

The bleak landscape here is often described as lunar and it was the site for some of the filming for *Planet of the Apes* in 1966.

El Teide – Spain's highest mountain

the park. Arrive early at the Teleférico to avoid queues and be aware that it does not operate in windy weather (book online at www.volcanolife.com). **El Teide**, the highest mountain in Spain, is 3,718m (12,198ft) above sea level and is extremely cold. Snow caps it for most of the year.

Most people who alight from the cable car do not want to walk far, and anyone who suffers from coronary or respiratory problems should not attempt to do so, as there is 50 percent less oxygen in the air here than at sea level. You can walk to the rim of the crater, but you need a permit. They are available free from the Parque Nacional office, Calle Sixto Perera González 25, La Orotava (tel: 922 922 371; Mon–Fri 9am–2pm) or at www.reservasparquesnacionales.es. You will need your passport and you will also need to show it at the summit.

El Teide rises from a great hollow, a *caldera*, that is the remnant of an earlier, much larger volcano. In fact there were two earlier volcanoes, creating two *calderas*, separated by the extraordinary gnarled formations of **Los Roques de García**, close to the *parador*. Lava and ashes have spilled from the volcanoes in a series of eruptions at different times, which explains why the rocks are so varied in texture and colour. Some are deep green from copper oxide, and are known as **Los Azulejos** (The Tiles).

A left turn at the **Mirador Boca de Tauce** a little further on leads to the village of Vilaflor. Or you could continue to the Mirador de Chío for a stark, cindery view of **Las Narices del Teide** (El Teide's Nostrils) created by an eruption in 1798.

The East

Candelaria, about 17km (11 miles) south of Santa Cruz, is a town with deep religious roots. It is dominated by the over-sized 1950s' **basilica** (open Tue–Sun 7.30am–7.30pm, Mon 3–7.30pm; free), containing an image of the Virgin, who, according to legend, was washed ashore here and worshipped by the Guanches, well before Christianity came to the Canaries. The statue and an earlier church were destroyed in 1826 when a tidal wave reclaimed the Virgin, the patron saint of the Canary Islands. The splendid new statue is the object of a major two-day pilgrimage in mid-August, the **Romería de Nuestra Señora de la Candelaria**, when the conversion of the Guanches to Christianity is re-enacted. Lining the sea side of the basilica's square are statues of the seven Guanche *menceys*, or chiefs, who were in power at the time of the Spanish conquest.

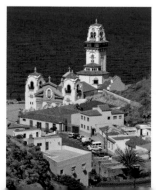
Candelaria's basilica

Parque Etnográfico Pirámides de Güímar

Just south and inland from Candelaria is the little working town of **Güímar**. Some of the dry stone terraces around the town, known as *molleros* or *majones*, look like the bases of pyramids and it is no surprise to find the **Parque Etnográfico Pirámides de Güímar** (open daily 9.30m–6pm; www. piramidesdeguimar.es) above the town. This park is the work of Thor Heyerdahl, who lived in Tenerife from 1994 until his death in 2002. During that time Heyerdahl, who had done extensive research on the pyramids of Tucume in Peru, discovered what he believed to be the Guanches' cult of building flat-topped, step-sided pyramids for sun worship, similar to those that have been found on both sides of the Atlantic.

Shipowner and fellow Norwegian, Fred Olsen, bought the land for the park and helped to develop it into a centre of research. On view are models of Heyerdahl's vessels, a video detailing his summaries and trans-oceanic crossings and various other audio-visual displays, as well as the pyramids themselves.

Costa Adeje

There is still controversy about the authenticity of the pyramids, but it is well worth visiting the site and deciding for yourself.

The South Coast

The most popular tourist destinations in Tenerife are the adjacent resorts of **Los Cristianos** and **Playa de las Américas**. The former used to be a small fishing port with a quiet little beach. It now plays host to hundreds of thousands of visitors each year. Traces of the old town can still be found around the port, though it is difficult to locate anything but British or German bars and restaurants along the crowded beachfront. The port is still active, its ferries serving the neighbouring islands of El Hierro and La Gomera. The south-facing **Playa los Cristianos** and **Playa de las Vistas** are sheltered, and the sea shallow and safe.

Los Cristianos is separated from its neighbour by the volcanic cone of Montaña Chayofila. Playa de las Américas was born in the 1970s and quickly developed from a bare shoreline to the high-rise, high-energy, highly packaged resort it is today. It has no natural centre or heart, the roads are often not signposted and directions are generally given by the names of hotels. A large beach, the Playa de Las Vistas, lies between the ambitious **Mare Nostrum** hotel resort and Los Cristianos, but the main beaches of **Playas de Troya** and **Playa del Bobo** are on the north side of the **Barranco del Rey**, which is near the rowdy strip called **Veronicas**, hub of more than 100 discos and nightclubs.

On the other side of Playa de las Américas is **Costa Adeje**. Here, the wall-to-wall hotels, fast-food joints and amusement arcades give way to spacious, cleverly designed resort hotels offering extensive facilities and creating a more agreeable ambience.

The small harbour of **Puerto Colón** in San Eugenio is the centre for water-based activities – glass-bottomed boat trips, and dolphin- and whale-watching boats. From the Marina San Miguel, further south, at the Costa del Silencio, the **Yellow Submarine** will take you under the ocean on a 45-minute trip that is especially interesting when it passes wrecks on the sea bed which have become a haven for fish, notably an array of huge stingrays. Inland from the port is **Aqualand**, a large waterpark (see page 98).

EL HIERRO

El Hierro, the smallest and most southwesterly of the Canary Islands, with an area of 280 sq km (110 sq miles), is in the administrative province of Santa Cruz de Tenerife. It has the highest density of volcanoes in the archipelago. Although the last eruption was over 200 years ago and the activity of a submarine volcano in 2011 hasn't provoked any damages, the inhabitants are well aware of the danger – there are more than 500 cones on the surface, with an additional 300 covered by lava flows. The island has no good beaches, but it is quiet

El Hierro's dramatic coast

and unspoiled – and some of the scenery is extraordinarily dramatic. A road links the airport, the port and the capital, Valverde, then crosses the island to El Golfo; a road tunnel links the capital with Frontera. Minor roads lead to most points of interest, but none go all the way round the coast. Visitors arrive at the airport on domestic flights from Tenerife or Gran Canaria, or by boat at Puerto de la Estaca.

Exploring the Island

Both entry points are close to **Valverde**, the only Canarian capital located inland, which was built 700m (2,300ft) above sea level to protect it from pirate raids. It is a small town, centred around the church of Nuestra Señora de la Concepción. There's not a lot to see – although you could visit the **Casa de las Quinteras** (open Mon–Fri 9am–2pm, Sat 10am–6pm; free) to see local crafts and industry – but there's a cheerful atmosphere, with bars and restaurants. You can get a bus from the bus station to other parts of the island. If you are driving, you could take the scenic route over the high spine of the island, across the *meseta*, to the farming town of San Andrés, then on to the clifftop **Mirador de la Peña** at the northern end of **El Golfo**. The cliffs were once part of an immense volcanic crater, but some 50,000 years ago one side of it slid into the sea, leaving behind a fertile valley and a gigantic bay. From the *mirador* restaurant, designed by César Manrique, there are dramatic views.

Alternatively, drive through the Moncanal tunnel from Valverde to **Frontera**, a village that is known mainly for its church of Nuestra Señora de la Candelaria, with a free-standing bell tower set on a volcanic cone, and the adjacent *lucha canaria* stadium. On the coast close by is the **Lagartario** (daily 10am–6pm), where some of El Hierro's giant lizards *(galliota simonyi)* are cared for, and the **Ecomuseo de Guinea** daily 10am–6pm), a restored village that shows developments in rural dwellings from the time of the Spanish conquest to the 20th century. Another attraction is **Cueva de Guinea**, a volcanic cave (guided tours only).

West of here lie the pretty village of **Sabinosa**, the remote Santuario de Nuestra Señora de los Reyes, and **El Sabinal**, a forest of juniper trees *(sabinosas)*, twisted, gnarled and bent by the wind. Close by is **Punta Orchilla**, the site of the zero meridian before it was transferred to Greenwich in the 19th century (see page 15). From here a road leads to the best beach, **Playa del Verodal**.

To reach the southeastern point of the island, return to the central axis then drop down through gentle pastures and pine woods to the village of **El Pinar**, known

Divers' paradise

In 2000, El Hierro and its surrounding waters were declared a Biosphere Reserve by Unesco. All sea life within the reserve is protected. This, combined with dramatic underwater features, makes it the best scuba diving spot in Spain.

for ceramics and jewellery. The route then runs through inhospitable volcanic clinker to **La Restinga**, a fishing village with a black sand beach, a diving centre and some good fish restaurants that has become one of the island's highlights after the eruption of a submarine volcano in 2011. The neighbouring **Bahía de Naos** is a marine nature reserve.

LA GOMERA

The circular island of **La Gomera**, also part of the province of Santa Cruz de Tenerife, is 378 sq km (147 sq miles) with a population of 20,720, twice that of El Hierro. It is a rugged, mountainous island, accessed by long, winding roads. The coastline is dominated by dramatic cliffs, with few beaches, and the interior is full of vertiginous, mostly verdant valleys, lined with narrow fields stepped into the mountainsides. These valleys are often covered by a ceiling of cloud, whisked in by the trade winds. In the centre, the Parque Nacional de Garajonay (see page 47), is a dense area of forest and fauna. In fact, a third of this little island has been divided into 17 Unesco-designated protected areas.

La Gomera is reached by ferry or domestic flights from neighbouring islands. The airport is in the south, near Playa de Santiago, the port is San Sebastián, the island's capital.

San Sebastián

San Sebastián de La Gomera (pop. 8.668) is a small town, known as the place where Columbus stopped to stock up with fresh food and water before leaving the known world in September 1492. At the **Plaza de las Américas**, a pavement mosaic shows the route of Columbus's voyage and next to the large tree is the Casa de la Aduana (Customs House; Mon–Fri 10am–6pm). It is said that Columbus drew water from the well here and took it to the New World. Leading off the square, the

San Sebastián

Calle del Medio, the only street of any consequence, features more connections with the great navigator. The **Iglesia Nuestra Señora de la Asunción**, built between 1490 and 1510, looks and feels so old that you can easily imagine Columbus praying in a dark recess, as a plaque here tells us he did, in 1492. Nearby there is the **Museo Arqueológico de la Gomera** (open winter Mon–Fri 10am–6pm, Sat–Sun 10am–2pm, summer till 7pm; www.museoslagomera.es), which offers a good insight into the island's history. A little way up the street is the modest **Casa de Colón** (open Mon–Fri 10am–6pm; free; www.museoslagomera.es), which is supposedly where the navigator stayed while in La Gomera. It displays some pre-Columbian pottery from Latin America and items relating to Columbus's voyage.

The North

The road from San Sebastián climbs steeply and the views soon become quite dizzying. The highest peak on La Gomera,

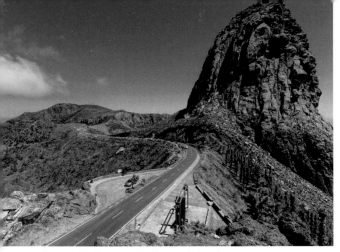

A road winds across La Gomera's interior

Alto de Garajonay is 1,487m (4,878ft) – this is no great height by Canaries standards, yet the island often gives the impression of being a fearsome maze of eerie crags. The small town of **Hermigua** is the largest on the island after San Sebastián. There is an interesting ethnographic museum presenting local crafts (open winter Mon–Fri 10am–6pm, Sat–Sun 10am–2pm, summer till 7pm; www.museoslago mera.es). Stop at the crafts centre of **Los Telares** (Mon–Sat 9am–12.30pm, 2–4.30pm; www.apartamentosgomera.com/molinodegofio) to look down into its green and fertile valley and ask if you can try the local liqueur, *mistela*. Also visit the handicrafts and delicatessen shop and the small private museum with a reconstructed water mill. Next comes **Agulo**, a pleasant little town perched precipitously on a headland. Its main feature (part from the location) is the domed Iglesia San Marco, originally a mosque, which stands beside a monumental laurel tree in the plaza.

A turn inland just before the village of Las Rosas takes you into the **Parque Nacional de Garajonay**, (www.parques nacionalesdecanarias.com) which was declared a Unesco World Heritage Site in 1986. The **Juego de Bolas Visitors Centre** (open daily 9.30am–4.30pm) incorporates a small Ethnographic Museum and a herbal garden.

The road then continues through the 3,984-hectare (9,884-acre) park to a restaurant near **La Laguna Grande**, a hospitable, rough-and-ready sort of place, which is very popular with walkers. There are no views from here, except at Garajonay itself, and an almost perpetual mist clings to the ancient, moss-covered trees. As there is little rainfall on La Gomera the mist, spawned by the trade winds, assumes great ecological importance, having given life to this sub-tropical forest, which includes laurel, cedar, juniper and olive trees, swathed in ferns and epiphytes (non-parasitic plants that grow on other plants).

The South

Starting the trip south from San Sebastián, the road leads past three mighty volcanic plugs to the windy pass of **Degollada de Peraza**, which offers spectacular views to both north and

The Lady in the Tower

The Torre del Conde (Tower of the Count, Mon–Fri 10am–6pm; www. museoslagomera.es) lies to the west of San Sebastián's main square. It is named after Count Hernán Peraza, who was ambushed and murdered one night on a mountain pass by two Guanche chiefs as he returned from an assignation with a Guanche princess. His wife, Beatriz, took refuge in the tower and legend has it that she entertained Columbus here before he set off on his voyage of discovery. The building does not seem to have changed much since then.

south; this is where the road divides. Instead of going in the direction of Garajonay, turn left on an extremely winding road that leads to **Playa de Santiago** (and the airport).

Apart from San Sebastián this is one of the few waterside communities on the island. There is a small port and a pebbly little beach but the main event is to be found on the cliffs immediately to the east. Here, the Norwegian shipping magnate Fred Olsen has created the **Jardín Tecina**, (www.jardin-tecina.com) an upmarket resort, with accommodation in a series of Canarian-style villas.

Retrace your route, passing the airport, and at Igualero turn left (west) on to a minor road to Las Hayas. Stop in the village of **El Cercado** where ceramic items are still made in the traditional manner by hand, without a potter's wheel. You may be surprised by the prices, which are nearly as steep as the island's cliffs and valley. There is also a small museum dedicated to the pottery, the Centro de Interpretación de Las Loceras (Mon–Fri 10am–6pm, Sat–Sun 10am–2pm).

From Las Hayas continue along to the main road at Arure where, immediately after turning left, there is a small bodega selling wines from La Gomera and the rest of the Canary Islands. La Gomera has about 300 hectares (742 acres) of vineyards, mostly cultivated on uneven land with steep slopes and small terraces. A stop at the highest point, at the combined *mirador*/restaurant Escuela César Manrique, will give you stupendous views of the verdant Valle Gran Rey, a deep and fertile gorge that has been terraced and planted with a wide variety of fruit and vegetables, and has been colonised by laid-back northern Europeans seeking peace and tranquillity.

Where the valley reaches the sea, the pretty village of

Island delicacy

Guarapo is a delicacy of La Gomera. To make it, sap is extracted from the crown of the Canarian palm tree and gently heated until it forms a thick, dark, honey-like syrup.

La Calera, set on a hill, has a number of boutiques and restaurants; and the little town of **Valle Gran Rey** has a black-sand beach, a few bars and restaurants and a dive centre. Return through the valley, continue past Arure and then take a right turn at the T-junction which will lead you along the southern edge of the national park and back to San Sebastián.

The black-sand beach at Valle Gran Rey

LA PALMA

La Palma, the most north-westerly of the Canaries, has an area of 725 sq km (280 sq miles) and a population of 83,450. It has two nicknames – La Isla Bonita (The Beautiful Island) and La Isla Verde (The Green Island) and both are appropriate. Its statistics are impressive, too. The highest peak, Roque de los Muchachos, rises 2,423m (7,950ft) above sea level, making it the steepest island in the world in relation to its total area. It is also the only one of the Canary Islands to have any streams – even very small ones.

Santa Cruz de la Palma

Santa Cruz de la Palma, the island capital, is an appealing town – clean and bright with a mix of traditional and modern architecture side-by-side creating a pleasing atmosphere. Most people agree that it is the most attractive of the Canary Islands' capitals. The prestige of the town was such that, during the Renaissance era, it was the third most important port of the Spanish Empire, after Sevilla and Antwerp.

The heart of the town is the triangular **Plaza de España**, set a couple of streets in from the seafront on the Calle Real. On one side of the triangle is the **Iglesia Matriz de El Salvador** (Church of the Saviour), built in 1503. The intricate wooden panelled ceiling of this big stone church is a fine example of the *mudéjar* style, a mixture of Muslim and Christian-Gothic elements perfected by the Muslim craftsmen who chose to remain in Spain after the 15th-century reconquest.

Beside the church, the **Quinta Verde**, dating from 1618 but rebuilt in the 1920s, is the most notable of the splendid 18th-century colonial-style mansions. There are plans to open a museum inside dedicated to the famous feast of Our Lady of the Snows (see page 52). The longest side of the plaza's triangle is

La Bajada de la Virgen procession in Santa Cruz

taken up by the colonnaded **Ayuntamiento** (Town Hall), built
between 1559 and 1567 with stone brought from La Gomera;
this is considered the most important Renaissance building in
the Canary Islands. While the arches are Italian Renaissance, the
interior (which you are free to inspect) is Spanish colonial, with
formidable carved wooden ceilings and doors and a ceremonial
staircase with frescoes painted in the mid-20th century.

The **Calle Real** is a delightful street in which to stroll and
enjoy the ambience. At its southern end it takes on the improb-
able name of Calle O'Daly, after an Irish banana merchant
who settled on the island. On the parallel Avenida Marítimo,
you will find the wonderful row of old houses known as the
Casas de los Balcones. Built in the 19th century, they have
become symbolic of Santa Cruz. Colourful and characteristic,
with a Portuguese influence, they take their name from their
overhanging balconies; the houses facing the sea were once
used as lookout posts.

Among other points of interest is the **Iglesia de San Francisco**, in the square of the same name, with a *mudéjar* ceiling to
equal that in the church of El Salvador. The cloister now houses
the **Museo Insular** (open winter Mon–Sat 10am–8pm, Sun
10am–2pm, in summer only Mon–Sat 10am–7.30pm), with an
eclectic mixture of exhibits. At the end of Calle Pérez Brito is
El Barco de la Virgen, a life-size replica of Columbus's ship,
Santa María, which houses the **Museo Naval** (open Mon–Thur
9.30am–2pm, 4–7pm, Fri 9.30am–2pm).

Santa Cruz also has a colourful market, the **Mercado
Municipal**, selling local produce, as well as two castles, the
Castillo Real, in the town itself, and the Castillo de la Virgen,
on a promontory above.

Due to the steep, dorsal shape of the island there are only
two main island routes to follow: the loop south of the
Caldera de Taburiente and the loop north of it. The southern
route is the more interesting of the two.

Casas de los Balcones

The Southern Loop

Heading west from Santa Cruz the first stop of interest is **Las Nieves**, a village built on the mountainside. You will first come to a roadside bar, then the 17th-century **Real Santuario de Nuestra Señora de las Nieves** (Sanctuary of Our Lady of the Snows), repository of the venerated 14th-century terracotta image of the Virgen de las Nieves, who is said to have appeared in Rome during an August snowstorm. The Virgin is celebrated every year on 5 August, but every five years (2015, 2020, etc.) there is a special event, when the image is carried to Santa Cruz in a procession known as *La Bajada de la Virgen* (The Descent of the Virgin).

Heading west, the road dives into a tunnel cut through La Cumbre Nueva, the mountainous ridge that runs through the centre of the island. At the other side, you pass the Visitor Centre of the Parque Nacional de la Caldera de Taburiente (see page 55). The main road then continues west to **El Paso**, a sweet village with traditional houses surrounded by a riot of prickly pear cacti. The **Parque Paraíso de las Aves** (open daily 10am–5pm) lies just beyond. The park shelters endangered species of exotic birds and runs guided tours and educational programmes. The next place of interest, **Los Llanos de Aridane**, in the heart of a fertile valley, has some good Canarian architecture and lush, colourful gardens. It's also a site of a new **Museo Arqueológico** Benahoarita (Mon–Sat 9am–8pm, Sun 9am–2pm) presenting the rich heritage of the island and a small, but interesting **Casa Museo del Vino Las Manshas** (Wine Museum, Mon–Fri 9.30am–1.30pm, 4–6.30pm).

Before taking the road to the southern tip, make a short detour to the **Mirador El Time**, a lookout point and restaurant perched above a rift valley, where the views are stupendous; then drop down to **Tazacorte**, a pretty village and harbour with some good fish restaurants. This was the port where Alonso Fernández de Lugo, the Spanish conqueror, landed in 1492.

Take the main road south now, following the mountainside, to **Fuencaliente**, famous for its wines. A winding road, covered with flowers in spring, leads to the lighthouse, El Faro de Fuencaliente, at the most southerly tip of La Palma. The first stop is at the **Bodegas Carballo** (open daily 11am–8pm; tel: 922 444 140; www.bodegascarballo.com), where you can sample and purchase some surprisingly strong local wines.

In 1677, the nearby volcano, San Antonio, erupted, covering once-fertile land with ash, leaving a layer of lapilli approximately 2m (6.5ft) deep. By the end of that century, farmers had developed a technique of digging trenches that enabled them to reach the fertile layer of earth under the cinders, where they planted the vines and then covered them with the extracted ashes. This

Explosive island

La Palma is the most active of the volcanic Canary Islands. The most recent eruption was by southern Teneguia in 1971. Extremely high temperatures can still be detected slightly below the surface.

Hiking along the volcano route

somehow allowed the plants to resist adverse weather conditions and even *phylloxera*, the plant louse that destroyed vines all over Europe in the late 19th century.

Just across the road you can stop at the edge of the crater of **Volcán de San Antonio** (Visitor Centre open daily 9am–6pm, in summer till 8pm) and visit the *mirador* beyond it. In an exposed, windy location this looks quite benign, considering the damage it did. Just south of here are even more recent signs of volcanic activity; the volcano of **Teneguía** that erupted in 1971, fortunately without human casualties. These eruptions sent an ever-widening stream of molten lava rushing down the hillside here and you can see it now, petrified and black, as the road runs right through it. Surprisingly, *plátanos* (bananas) seem to like this environment and are growing all around. (For a history of banana growing on the islands, visit the small **Banana Museum**; Camino San Antonio, El Charco, Tazacorte; open Mon–Fri 10am–1pm, 4–7pm, Sun and Sat by appointments only; tel: 922 480 803).

Back at sea level, you will find the **Playa de Zamora**, a small beach of jet-black sand squeezed between the surreal lava fields. A short distance away, next to the twin lighthouses, is a little fishermen's cove with a stony beach where there is a tiny restaurant serving delicious fried fresh fish.

Heading back towards Santa Cruz, stop at the **Parque Arqueológico de Belmaco** (open Mon–Sat 10am–6pm, Sun 10am–3pm). The first stone engravings found in the Canary Islands were discovered here in the 18th century, and the 10 natural cave dwellings, with their magnificent rock engravings, were the home to the Benahoritas – the ancient settlers of Benahoare, which is the aboriginal name for La Palma.

A little further on is **Mazo**, the place to buy authentic-looking replicas of the aboriginal pots, as well as locally made cigars – *puros*. At Corpus Christi (May/June) the streets of Mazo are covered in patterned carpets of flowers, leaves and sand.

The Northern Loop

The serpentine road up the east coast runs through some pretty scenery, and you can stop at the **Mirador de San Bartolomé** for beautiful vistas along the coast in both directions. Head next for the seaside village of **San Andrés** with natural swimming pools nearby at **El Charco Azul** (The Blue Pool). A little way inland from San Andrés is the **Bosque de Los Tiles**, a large wooded area that preserves some of the Canary Islands' original, and much depleted, laurel forest. It is a designated Biosphere Reserve under the protection of Unesco. There's a Visitor Centre (open Mon–Fri 8.30am–5.30pm) that can provide maps and information on walking trails.

The main reason to visit the northern part of the island, however, is to experience the **Parque Nacional de la Caldera de Taburiente**. The Visitor Centre (open daily 9am–6pm; www.parquesnacionalesdecanarias.com) is outside the park itself, on the road to El Paso (see page 52). They have information on the geology and geomorphology, flora and fauna, and helpful hints on camping as well as a useful coloured diagram of the hiking trails. The Caldera de Taburiente is a giant crater, measuring 1,500m (1,640yds) deep, with a diameter of 10km (6 miles). It was created some 400,000 years ago and has since been colonised by nature into a green, fertile valley.

From the Visitor Centre you can drive 7km (4 miles) to the **Mirador La Cumbrecita**, on a road that climbs into a craggy forest surrounded by mist-shrouded peaks with tall pines clinging to precarious ledges. There are wonderful views from here (weather permitting – which it doesn't most of the time), including the Roque de los Muchachos and the monolithic Roque Idafe, said to have been the sacred altar of the first Guanche natives on the island. You can enjoy the Caldera by car, but to get the most from the area you have to walk.

Approaching from the north, by road, you must take the turning just outside Santa Cruz that snakes past the Pico de las Nieves to the **Roque de los Muchachos**, the highest point in the island at 2,426m (7,960ft) above sea level. There are several ways up to it, but always be aware of the weather; what looks fine from sea level takes on a different perspective at this height. And, of course, it can change dramatically and quickly, so go prepared with wet-weather gear, warm layers and strong shoes. Besides the views, the other attraction up here is the futuristic **Observatorio Astrofísico** (closed to visitors except for special days in the summer announced on the website www.iac.es), regarded as the most important observatory in the Northern Hemisphere and home to some of the world's most important telescopes, including the 400-cm (157-in) William Herschel telescope.

From the observatory, the road continues northwest to the isolated community of **Santo Domingo de Garafía**, where fierce waves lash the rocky coast.

The bright lights of Las Palmas

GRAN CANARIA

Gran Canaria, the third-largest island in the archipelago, has a great combination of perfect beaches, cultural sites, dramatic scenery, lively nightlife and seriously good restaurants. It is almost circular in shape, with an area of 1,530 sq km (590 sq miles) and a coastline of 235km (145 miles), of which more than a fifth consists of beaches. Gran Canaria is the classic volcanic cone in profile and its mountainous character causes the climate to change radically with latitude and altitude. You can leave a damp and cloudy Las Palmas in the early morning and an hour later be enjoying blazing hot sun in Maspalomas.

Gran Canaria is known as a continent in miniature. The coastline ranges from awe-inspiring cliffs to golden dunes. Inland, it varies between stark mountains and tranquil valleys. To preserve this diversity, 32 protected areas cover nearly 43 percent of the island's surface.

Las Palmas

Bustling **Las Palmas** (population 382,000 – the largest city in the Canaries), is a major commercial and historical centre, a cosmopolitan resort and a vital seaport all rolled into one.

The northern hub of Las Palmas is the **Parque Santa Catalina**, palm-dotted and full of outdoor cafés, buzzing by day and night. On the port side of the park is the striking **Museo Elder** (open Tues–Sun 10am–8pm; www.museoelder.org), a wonderful and well-organised science and technology museum. A landscaped pedestrian area leads from the museum, past an enormous, sail-like awning, beneath which is the city's subterranean bus terminal, to the **Muelle Santa Catalina** where a shiny commercial centre in brilliant shades of blue and yellow, **El Muelle** (www.ccelmuelle.es), houses stores, cinemas, discos and open-air restaurants and cafés. It is a short walk from the other side of the square to **Playa de las Canteras**, a 3-km (2-mile) stretch of sand that made the city Gran Canaria's first tourist resort, although it has been losing its younger tourist trade to the resorts in the south, It is lined with hotels and restaurants, some of which have been here since the 1960s heyday. A wide promenade runs the length of the beach, and a natural reef, **La Barra**, a few hundred metres out, turns this stretch into a natural lagoon, safe for children and non-swimmers.

Take a bus back from Santa Catalina to **Parque Doramas**, a pleasantly landscaped park named after a Guanche chieftain, surrounding the Hotel Catalina. Adjacent to it is the **Pueblo Canario**, a romanticised version of a Canarian village where you can shop for handicrafts and watch displays of folk dancing and singing (Sun 11.30am; free). It was designed by the local Modernist artist, Néstor Fernández de la Torre (1887–1938), and his architect brother, Miguel. The **Museo Néstor** (Mon–Sat 10am–7pm, Sun 10.30am–2.30pm) displays many of his paintings and stage designs. Further south on Calle Alfonso XIII, is the beautiful blue building of the **Casa Africa** (exhibitions Mon–Fri 10am–6.30pm; www.casafrica.es), which promotes African culture and celebrates relations between the three continents of Europe, Africa and South America.

Further south is **Parque San Telmo**, where the city's main (underground) bus terminal, a pretty little chapel, the Ermita de San Telmo, and an Art Nouveau refreshment kiosk, decorated with gleaming tiles, marks the start of **Triana**, one of the older *barrios* (districts). The long, pedestrianized shopping street of Calle Mayor de Triana, has attractive Art Nouveau façades and a wide

Playa de las Canteras

variety of shops. The **Casa-Museo Pérez Galdós** (open Tues–Sun 10am–6pm; www.casamuseoperezgaldos.com) pays homage to the writer born here in 1843 and known as the Spanish Balzac. The house is a delightful example of Canarian architecture.

Close by are two pretty squares, the **Plazoleta de Cairasco**, with the splendid **Gabinete Literario** (www.gabineteliterario. com), an Art Nouveau treasure designated a 'Monumento Histórico Artístico'; and Hurtado de Mendoza, usually known as **Las Ranas** (The Frogs) because the long pool that runs down the centre is fed by two spouting frogs.

Cross the major highway, Calle Juan de Quesada, and you reach **Vegueta**, the oldest part of the city, where Spanish forces first set up camp in 1478. It is claimed that Christopher Columbus prayed at the **Ermita de San Antonio Abad** before setting off to the New World. This pretty area has some magnificent colonial architecture and cobbled streets, brightened up with bursts of bougainvillaea. It comes alive at night, with many bars and *tascas* open until the early hours.

Close by on Calle Colón is the beautiful, 15th-century **Casa de Colón** (open Mon–Sat 10am–6pm, Sun 10am–3pm; www.casadecolon.com). This was the residence of the island's first governor and Columbus is said to have stayed here, although there is no evidence to support this. Now an atmospheric museum, with a pretty courtyard, it recreates the Age of Discovery with exhibits of navigational instruments, charts and weapons, a replica of the cabin of *La Niña*, one of Columbus's ships and pre-Columbian artefacts from Mexico and the Ecuadorian island of La Tolita.

Casa de Colón

Around the corner stands the vast bulk of the **Catedral de Santa Ana** (open Mon–Fri 10am–4.30pm, Sat 10am–1.30pm; access only through the Diocesan Museum; www.diocesisdecanarias.es), a mixture of Gothic, Renaissance and neoclassical styles. The adjoining **Museo Diocesano de Arte Sacro** (open

as above; entrance in Calle Espíritu Santo) has a lovely cloister, the Patio de los Naranjos (Patio of the Orange Trees), its tranquillity disturbed only by birdsong. A modern lift will whisk you up to the top of one of the cathedral's two towers for a great view over the city. Facing the cathedral across the **Plaza de Santa Ana** are the splendid Casas Consistoriales (Island Government Offices).

Not far away, the **Centro Atlántico de Arte Moderno (CAAM)** (open Tue–Sat 10am–9pm, Sun 10am–2pm; www.caam.net) focuses on the work of young Canarian artists. The nearby **Museo Canario** (open Mon–Fri 10am–8pm, Sat–Sun 10am–2pm; www.elmuseocanario.com; free entrance Mon and Wed 5–7pm) holds the islands' most important collection of pre-Hispanic objects, including a room full of Cro-Magnon skulls and mummies. Further east, at Ramón y Cajal 1, in a beautifully refurbished 18th-century former hospital, is the San Martín Centro de la Cultura Contemporánea (open Tue–Sat 10am–9pm, Sun 10am–2pm; www.sanmartincontemporaneo.com), a modern art gallery space and concert hall.

The East Coast

Heading down the motorway (GC-1) past the airport to the southern beaches, it is worth stopping off at the **Barranco**

de Guayadeque. The *barranco* is one of the most beautiful valleys on the island, its steep slopes are honeycombed with cave dwellings, and lush flora thrives here. The **Museo de Guayadeque and Centro de Interpretación Arqueologica** (open Tue–Sat 9am–5pm, Sun 10am–3pm) has lots of displays on its history and will give information on hiking trails. The *barranco* is for serious walkers, but the less energetic can drive for some 9km (5 miles) beyond the museum, passing glorious scenery, to reach two cave villages, both still viable communities. The road ends at one of several cave bars and restaurants, the **Tagoror** (www.restaurantetagoror.com).

Nearby, **Agüimes** is one of the most appealing towns on the island. Among the ochre- and terracotta-coloured houses in the spotless, narrow streets, a number of bronze statues have been erected, portraying rural life and local characters. Several houses have been converted into *casa rural* accommodation (see page 116). The neoclassical **Iglesia de San Sebastián** (open daylight hours) and the Museo de Historia de Agüimes (Tue–Sun 9am–5pm) at Calle Juan Alvarado y Saz, 42, are definitely worth a visit.

The Count's Vision

The Conde del Castillo de la Vega Grande de Guadelupe, an aristocrat with a pedigree as long as his name, once had a family home in Telde, in a building that is now the town hall. He also owned large tracts of unused and seemingly useless land in the barren south of the island. In the early 1960s, as the tourist boom swept through mainland Spain, the Count came up with a scheme that would change the face and the economy of Gran Canaria. Out of the desert, he constructed what are now the resorts of San Agustín, Playa del Inglés and Maspalomas. Tour companies, quick to spot a potential gold mine, soon moved building contractors in. Within two decades the south of Gran Canaria had developed into a huge holiday complex.

A short way from Agüimes are **Playa de Vargas** and **Pozo Izquierdo**, venues for the annual PWA Windsurf Championships; and a marine reserve and diving centre, at **Playa del Cabrón**.

Southern Resorts

The southern resorts of San Agustín, Playa del Inglés and Maspalomas, the biggest holiday complex in Spain, are synonymous with package holidays. Built in the 1960s to provide instant gratification,

Among the Maspalomas dunes

they offer year-round good weather, miles of rolling sands, water sports facilities, hotels and apartments with lush gardens and landscaped swimming pools; and restaurants, clubs, bars and shops by the score.

San Agustín, the first resort you reach on the GC-1 motor-way, is a relatively restrained area of apartment complexes, catering mainly for retired couples and families with young children, although it is also extremely popular with windsurf-ers. You can walk along the promenade to **Playa del Inglés**, a far louder and more robust resort. The name means English Beach, but it attracts numerous German visitors as well. This is a sprawling sun, sea and sand resort of high-rise hotels, shop-ping malls, amusement arcades and fast-food restaurants. The nightlife at the numerous discos, bars and clubs can be hectic and lasts till the early hours.

Maspalomas is separated from Playa del Inglés by a spec-tacular stretch of **dunes** that cover an area of 4 sq km (1.5 sq miles) and were designated a nature reserve in 1994. You can

Puerto de Mogán

walk over the dunes if you protect your feet from the hot sand, but it is hard going and takes over an hour. Following the beach around takes half the time, and you will pass a popular nudist stretch en route. Adjoining the dunes, a golf course forms another barrier, but inland the two resorts almost merge into each other, although their style is distinctive. Maspalomas is a more upmarket resort and accommodation is in smart hotels, bungalows or low-rise apartment complexes set in large, lush gardens. Playa de Maspalomas is the stretch of dunes close to **El Faro**, the lighthouse. From here a palm-lined *paseo* leads to the area known as **El Oasis**, which has some smart hotels and other more affordable apartments, beside **La Charca**, a small lagoon.

There is a plethora of family attractions nearby, all reached by regular bus services from the resorts (see What to Do). West of Maspalomas the coastline becomes dominated by towering, barren looking cliffs that form natural bays and coves. The motorway continues to Puerto Rico, but the coast road passes

Pasito Blanco, a little port and resort, which is mainly of interest to sailing enthusiasts; and **Arguineguín**, a working fishing port that has expanded into a busy tourist resort.

Puerto Rico is the next major resort on this coast. Conceived in the 1970s, it has been somewhat overdeveloped, with a wall of apartment blocks rising to the top of the hills, like tiers of seats in a giant amphitheatre. Its pretty, sheltered beach is clean and family-orientated but can become unbearably crowded. The *Puerto Deportivo* (or leisure harbour) caters for fishing and water-sports enthusiasts and for those who just like being on the water. There are diving schools and sailing schools, deep-sea fishing trips, 'dolphin search' trips in glass-bottomed catamarans, as well as simple pleasure trips that run up and down the coast.

A little further west, **Puerto de Mogán** is a lesson in how to provide accommodation that is functional, attractive and totally in sympathy with its surroundings. Built round a complex of sea-water canals with delicately arched bridges, the modern versions of traditional local townhouses are ablaze with bougainvillaea and trailing geraniums. There are two harbours, the working one, from which a fishing fleet still operates; and the *Puerto Deportivo*, where luxurious yachts bob in the water. The latter is lined with cafés and restaurants, all offering wonderful views and fish and seafood menus, all fairly similar. There is a small, south-facing beach to the east of the harbour, that has recently been 'sandscaped' and extended. **Atlantida Submarine** offers trips in a yellow submarine (see page 89) and pleasure boats ply back and forth between here, Puerto Rico and Arguiniguín.

Northern Coast and Hinterland

Going west from Las Palmas on the motorway, take the exit for **Arucas**, a workaday town overshadowed by the huge lava-stone church of **San Juan Bautista**; begun in 1909, it is said to owe its inspiration to Antoni Gaudí's Sagrada Família in Barcelona.

Roque Nublo at sunset

The road west from Arucas follows a dizzying route through the mountains, but you can return to the coast road or motorway, and make a detour to **Moya**, a pretty little town with an impressive church, precariously perched on the edge of a ravine.

Just off the coast road is the **Cenobio de Valerón** (open winter Tue–Sun 10am–5pm, summer till 6pm; www.arqueologia canaria.com). *Cenobio* means convent, and this complex of about 300 caves, hollowed out of the soft, volcanic rock, was believed to have been a place where young women were detained in order to protect their virginity until they married. However, it is now widely accepted that the caves were actually grain stores.

Stop at **Gáldar**, which is also known as the Ciudad de los Guanartemes, as it was once the Guanche capital. The **Iglesia de Santiago de los Caballeros**, in a shady square, was built on the spot where chief Semidan's palace supposedly stood. The **Museo y Parque Arqueologico Cueva Pintada** (Painted Cave Museum and Archaeological Park; open Jun–Sept

Tue–Sat 10.30am–7.30pm, Sun 11am–7pm, Oct–May Tue–Sat 10am–6pm, Sun 11am–6pm; www.cuevapintada.com), is the main Guanche site, close to the centre of town, with walls covered with their colourful, geometric paintings, discovered in the second half of the 19th century.

Now go south towards **Agaete**, the most attractive of the northern towns. It stands on the edge of the **Barranco de Agaete**, a beautiful, fertile valley, usually signposted simply as El Valle. The road goes up to the viewpoint at the village of **Los Berrazales**. Agaete's port, **Puerto de las Nieves**, is a haven of calm among the formidable rocky cliffs that make up this stretch of coast. There's a sweet church, the Ermita de las Nieves, and a new jetty has been built in the harbour, where a number of good fish restaurants line the quay and ferries depart for Santa Cruz de Tenerife.

The road along the west coast winds through barren rocks on one side and sheer cliffs on the other. Keep your eyes on the road until you reach one of the two look-out points, the **Andén Verde** and the **Mirador del Balcón**, both with superlative views along the craggy coastline and across the sea.

Central Sights

The mountainous centre of the island is tiring to drive around, but the wonderful panoramas are ample reward. Pine forests, almond groves, gnarled mountains, sheer cliffs and cloudy mountain tops beckon.

The best and most popular vantage point is the **Cruz de Tejeda**, the sombre stone cross marking the top of a pass, at 1,580m (5,184ft). This is one of the few points inland where you are almost guaranteed to meet fellow tourists. Restaurants (one, El Refugio, is also a hotel; www.hotelruralelrefugio.com), fruit and souvenir stalls and men offering donkey rides make it a hive of activity. The magnificent panorama includes two rock formations that were once worshipped by the Guanches.

One is the **Roque Bentaiga** (1,412m/4,632ft), the other, the most distinctive, is the statuesque bulk of **Roque Nublo** at 1,803m (5,915ft). It takes little imagination to understand the early inhabitants' fascination with these stark, brooding peaks.

The Cruz de Tejeda is the hub of the island, and there are any number of routes to it, so you could go up one way and down another. From Las Palmas, the most northerly route runs through the peaceful town of **Teror**. The whitewashed houses, many built around graceful patios, have traditional carved balconies. The **Basílica de Nuestra Señora del Pino** (Our Lady of the Pine Tree; open Mon–Fri 11am–3pm, Sun 11am–2pm, 3.30–5.45pm; www.basilicadelpino.es) commemorates a vision of the Virgin in the branches of a pine tree, seen by shepherds in 1481.

The Virgen del Pino is the most popular saint on the island and a huge festival is held in her honour during the first week of September. Beside the church, the **Museo de Los Patronos de la Virgen del Pino** (open Mon–Fri 11am–6pm, Sun 10am–2pm) in a beautiful building, set around a courtyard, is furnished in the style of a noble, 17th-century home.

An alternative route from Las Palmas, through the suburbs of Santa Brígida and Vega de San Mateo, passes close to the **Caldera de Bandama**, a green and fertile volcanic crater, almost 1km (0.5 mile) across and some 200m (655ft) deep. The views from here take in the mountains, the fertile valley and vast stretches of the coastline.

You can also reach the central area via an extremely winding but beautiful route from Moya via **Artenara**, the highest village on the island, where the houses are built into the solid rock. There is a cave church and a cave

Humble advice

A sign in the Basilica de Nuestra Señora del Pino, in Teror, reads: 'Although the Virgin is grateful for your gifts and candles she would rather you gave your money to the poor.'

restaurant, the **Méson La Silla**, entered through a tunnel, where you can get good, substantial, island food.

LANZAROTE

Lanzarote is the fourth-largest island in the Canaries, with an area of 805 sq km (310 sq miles) and a population of almost 142,000. It is a startling place, representing the triumph of civilisation over a hostile environment; the entire island has been declared a Biosphere Reserve by Unesco. Its pock-marked, lunar surface, 60km (37 miles) long and 20km (12.5miles) wide, is dotted with more than 300 volcanoes, yet onions, pot-

One of Playa Blanca's inviting beaches

atoes, tomatoes, melons and grapes all spring in abundance from the black ash. Lanzarote's most unusual farm crop, however, is the cochineal beetle that, when crushed, emits a red dye used as colouring for Campari and lipstick (see page 20). Newer to the tourist scene than either Gran Canaria or Tenerife, Lanzarote has learned from the excesses of its sister islands. Here, small is beautiful and harmony with the environment is the philosophy.

The South

Arrecife, the principal port and latter-day capital, does not have a lot of character. It has two interesting historical buildings. The first is the 16th-century **Castillo de San Gabriel**, situated close to the centre of town. Closed for many years it now houses the **Museo de Historia de Arrecife**. It is worth the walk across the drawbridge and over the lagoon, on to the little island where the castle was set to deter pirates.

The **Castillo de San José**, a few kilometres to the north, is far more interesting. Built in the 18th century, this well-preserved fortress once guarded the harbour. It now houses the late César Manrique's compact but impressive **Museo de Arte Contemporáneo** (open daily 10am–8pm; Tue–Sat restaurant noon–4pm, Fri–Sat 7–11pm, bar daily 10am–8pm, Fri–Sat 9.30pm–1am; www.centrosturisticos.com). The museum displays works by Picasso and Miró, as well as Manrique himself, and is notable for the contrast between the modern exhibits and the ancient structure that houses them.

The island's major resort is **Puerto del Carmen**, about 10km (16 miles) south of Arrecife. Its long, golden beach stretches for 5km (3 miles) and comfortably accommodates its visitors. The sea is calm and ideal for children. Bars, shops and restaurants of every kind line the Avenida de las Playas, Lanzarote's one outbreak of mass commercialism.

The **old town** just west of the beach has an appealing small harbour area with traditional bars and restaurants and an array of marine adventures, such as glass-bottomed catamaran trips and sport-fishing charters.

Take the next turning left off the main road to reach **Puerto Calero**, which is dominated by a smart modern marina lined with good restaurants and blocks of expensive apartments. Boat and submarine trips are advertised in the marina, including one to Papagayo (see page 74).

The main road west leads through the beautifully tended village of **Yaiza**, with freshly painted houses and a profusion of flowers. Here, Manrique converted a farmhouse into a now-famous restaurant, La Era (www.laera.com). Between the villages of Uga and Yaiza is the entrance to the **Parque Nacional**

Camel ride in the Parque Nacional de Timanfaya

de Timanfaya (open daily 9am–4pm; www.parquesnacion-alesdecanarias.es), which encompasses the area known as **Montañas de Fuego** (Mountains of Fire). Just north of Yaiza, at a spot called **Echadero de Camellos** (open daily 9am–4pm) you can board a camel for a ride up the volcanic slopes of Timanfaya. This desolate area was formed by a series of eruptions in the 1730s, when the volcano was active for almost six years, and 11 villages were buried forever.

Drive on and turn left at the small roundabout to the Montañas del Fuego (daily 9am–5.45pm, in summer till 6.45pm; www.centrosturisticos.com). Your introduction to the inner sanctum of the mountains leaves no doubt that at least one of these volcanoes (the one you are standing on) is not dead, just sleeping. Less than 10m (32ft) beneath the surface the tempera-ture reaches 600°C (1,112°F) and at the surface level it can, at certain places, get to 120°C (248°F). A guide demonstrates this by pouring water down a tube into the earth, then retreating before a geyser of hot water erupts. In the nearby **Isolote de Hilario**, the restaurant El Diablo (daily 1–3.30pm), meat is grilled on heat rising directly from the ground – an instant, natural barbecue.

Cars are not allowed any further into the park and from here you must get into a coach to explore the incredible landscape. Any *malpaís* (badlands) that you may have seen up to this point have been a mere appetiser for the main course. The words *lunar* and *alien* are worked to exhaustion in attempts to describe the area and still scarcely do justice to the dramatic scenery. The last period of volcanic activity here began in 1824 and lasted 10 years.

The most impressive example of the local dry-farming method known as *enarenado* (see box) is the vineyards around the valley of **La Geria**. Each vine is set in its own mini-crater, protected from wind and excess sun by a low, semi-circular wall of lava stones (other crops are also protected in this manner). The horseshoe patterns thus formed stretch way up the mountains and apparently into infinity.

There are several *bodegas* in the Geria valley where you can sample the excellent local *malvasía*. Just outside **San Bartolomé** is the **Museo del Vino El Grifo** (open daily 10.30am–6pm; www.elgrifo.com), where there is a library of antique books. Manrique's monument to El Grifo adorns

Enarenado – Dry Cultivation

With rainfall so rare and underground water sources extremely limited, how does Lanzarote manage to survive as an agricultural island? The black topsoil is the secret: the porous volcanic particles that make up the topsoil are useless in themselves but act as a sponge for the moisture in the night air, obtaining water for the plants and eliminating the need for rain. The topsoil is piled on top of the crops and only needs replacing about once every 20 years. This method of dry cultivation is known as *enarenado* and is unique to Lanzarote.

the entrance to the bodega, the oldest in the Canaries, which has been producing wines since the 18th century. There are exhibitions of wine-making tools, and you can stroll through the vineyards and enjoy wine-tasting sessions. Also in San Bartolomé, the **Museo Etnográfico Tanit** (open Mon–Sat 10am–2pm; www.museotanit.com), chronicles Lanzarote's past.

Vines growing on black topsoil in La Geria wine country

The geographic centre of Lanzarote lies a short distance from San Bartolomé. Here, Manrique designed and erected a stark white sculpture, the **Monumento al Campesino**, dedicated to the peasant workers of the island. The interesting **Casa Museo del Campesino** (open daily 10am–5.45m, summer till 6.30pm; free) includes a restaurant (noon–4pm) that serves typical Canarian dishes.

Rejoin the main road now and go west, past Yaíza, where a right turn leads to the fishing village of **El Golfo**. Here, a placid, emerald-green lagoon lies beneath a cliff that resembles a gigantic, petrified tidal wave just about to break. This is the inner rim of a volcanic cone, half of which has disappeared beneath the sea. The strata, colours and whirls are fascinating. El Golfo is not apparent from the roadside; you have to park on the rough ledge, just off the main road as you begin the descent into the village (renowned for its fish restaurants) and follow the rough footpath over the cliff.

Drive on south to the natural lagoon, **Laguna de Janubio** and the salt flats called **Las Salinas de Janubio**. The coarse salt extracted here was once in great demand to preserve fish

Fundación César Manrique

caught in Arrecife. The demand is less now, but the flats still provide the salt that local artists dye a variety of colours and pour onto the streets of Arrecife in June, to create religious and secular designs for the Corpus Christi festivities.

The newish resort of **Playa Blanca** on the south coast, where the main road ends, is the third major tourist centre on the island. It is also the starting point for the Fuerteventura ferry (a 40-minute trip); there's a marina here, a good, golden beach and a number of hotels, restaurants and other facilities. However, just a few kilometres east are the best sands on the island, three beaches collectively known as the **Playas de Papagayo** (Parrot Beaches). The road is well-surfaced at first, but soon becomes exceedingly rough and rocky. There are few facilities on the beaches, so take a picnic, but you won't need much else, as nude bathing is the norm. There are boats that will drop you off here in the morning and return to pick you up in the afternoon, or take you on a round trip from Puerto Calero.

The North

On an island so dominated by the works and creativity of one man, it is essential to pay a visit to the **Fundación César Manrique** (open daily 10am–6pm; www.fcmanrique.org) at Tahiche, about 12km (7 miles) northwest of Arrecife. Manrique lived here and, as you might expect, it is rather unusual. Built in 1968 over a river of lava formed from the eruptions of the 1730s, it takes advantage, at its lowest point, of five volcanic bubbles to create the strange but impressive, minimalist living space.

You could make a detour across the island to **La Santa**, home of the Club La Santa (www.clublasanta.com), a time-share development resort where top-grade athletes come for training and relaxation. It offers its guests first-class facilities for every kind of sport imaginable. The windswept beaches along this stretch of the coast have views of the daunting cliffs of the Famara Massif that lead up to the Mirador del Río and Isla Graciosa (see page 78). Windsurfing is popular here, but the currents can be dangerous, so take care.

Alternatively, take the main road north from the Monumento de Campesino to **La Villa de Teguise**, a fine old town of cobbled streets and gracious mansions that was the island capital until 1852. The 15th-century parish church of **Nuestra Señora de Guadalupe** is the oldest on the island. Across the square the 16th-century **Convento de San Francisco** is now a museum of sacred art. On Sunday, a **handicrafts market** comes to town, where, among other things, you can buy a *timple* – a small ukulele-like instrument used by folkloric musicians. Several of the old buildings have been converted to craft and antique shops and restaurants. The **Convento de Santo Domingo**, at Guadalupe 18,

Uniform colours

Building materials and paint for external surfaces in Lanzarote are only available in brown, green and blue – the designated colours for any woodwork on the white buildings.

houses a gallery of contemporary art. High on top of an extinct volcano, the Montaña de Guanapay, overlooking the town, stands the 16th-century **Castillo Museo de Santa Bárbara**. The views from this wind-blown point alone are worth the trip. The castle now hosts the **Museo de la Piratería** (open daily 10am–4pm, winter Mon–Sat 9am–4pm; www.museodelapirateria.com), which brings to life the biggest raids experienced by the island by such famous pirates as John Hawkins, Francis Drake or Robert Blake.

You can drop down to the coast now, to **Costa Teguise**, around 10km (6 miles) north of Arrecife. This is a totally modern resort, comprising several *urbanizaciónes* with time-shares, hotels and apartments designed for a wealthy clientele. Early development was overseen by Manrique; later constructions are less tasteful. There is a handful of good sandy beaches, notably **Playa de las Cucharas**, where water sports thrive and windsurfing is popular. There is a championship golf course (see page 92) and the **Aquapark Costa Teguise** (open daily 10am–6pm; http://aquaparklanzarote.es) 2km (1 mile) inland.

The road up the east coast passes the town of **Guatiza**, where prickly pears abound and cochineal beetles are still cultivated. César Manrique also cultivated the spiny flora into

The Magic of Manrique

César Manrique, born here in 1919, was Lanzarote's greatest artist, designer, landscaper and conservationist. He died in a car crash in 1992 and is sorely missed. There is hardly a visitor attraction that does not bear his signature in some way. In his own words, his works were 'dreams that capture the sublime natural beauty of Lanzarote', and he tried to ensure that tourist developments were in harmony with the island's character. Simplicity was the key – whitewashed walls, natural building materials and ingenious water features are his hallmarks.

the beautiful **Jardín de Cactus** (open daily 10am–6pm, summer 9am–6pm; www.centrosturisticos.com) complete with a working windmill that produces its own *gofio* (see page 16). There is more Manrique design to admire at the caves of **Jameos del Agua** (open daily 10am–6.30pm; Sat in winter till 10pm and in summer till noon; www.centrosturisticos.com). Opened in 1966, this was the first visitor attraction Manrique designed, trans-

Jardín de Cactus

forming a grotto and underground lagoon into a short fantasy journey. Ethereal mood music accompanies your descent into the cave, lushly planted with luxuriant foliage. Peer into the black lagoon and you can pick out the very rare, tiny, blind, albino crabs, *Munidopsis polymorpha*, that live here. Resist the temptation to throw coins into the crystal clear lagoon; the corrosion of the metal kills the crabs. Finally you emerge from the cave into a South Seas paradise, complete with a swimming pool and landscaped terraces.

A museum here, the **Casa de los Volcanes** (open Mon–Fri 10am–6.30pm) is a study centre for volcanology. There is also a restaurant and bar.

The **Cueva de los Verdes** (open daily 10am–6pm, summer 10am–7pm; www.centrosturisticos.com) across the main road, is part of the same system and was blasted through the earth by exploding lava. There is a guided tour that includes some sound and light effects that evoke the menacing volcano most effectively.

Cueva de los Verdes

At the northern tip of the island is the small fishing port of **Orzola**. This is the embarkation point for a ferry service to the tiny **Isla Graciosa**, run by Líneas Maritimas Romero (www.lineasromero.com). With superb beaches and a complete lack of tourist development, this is the place to get away from it all for the day.

For an unforgettable view of Isla Graciosa drive up to the **Mirador del Río** (open daily 10am–6pm, summer 10am–7pm; www.centrosturi sticos.com), an observation gallery built into the cliff-side – yet another of César Manrique's unmissable creations. This is probably the most spectacular *mirador* in the Canaries. Great cliffs curve down to the beach, with Graciosa just across the strip of water called simply El Río (The River), and two smaller islands, Montaña Clara and Alegranza, in the background. Combined with a small section of the northwest coast of Lanzarote, the islands form the **Parque Nacional del Archipiélago Chinijo**. The only sound here is the wind gently whistling through El Río. Besides the huge picture windows in the *mirador*, note more of Manrique's creative sculptures in the bar/restaurant.

In the carefully landscaped gardens of **Las Pardelas Recreational Nature Park** (open 10am–6pm, summer 10am–7pm; for guided tours, tel: 928 842 545; www.pardelas-park.

com) near Guinate just south of the Mirador del Río (Ctra Orzola–Yé, Km1), you will find numerous species of indigenous plants, while children can visit the farm animals and have donkey rides.

FUERTEVENTURA

Fuerteventura is the second-largest island, at 2,020 sq km (780 sq miles), but it is an arid, windy and sparsely populated one. The population is just 106,930 and, despite a substantial amount of development in recent years, beaches still outnumber hotels. At the last count there were 152 beaches, many of them of fine, golden sand, the best selection in the Canary Islands. Fuerteventura's coastal shelf allows for shallow transparent waters that often acquire a beautiful turquoise colour. The island lies less than 115km (70 miles) off the North African coast, and most of the sand is blown here from the Sahara, giving a new meaning to the term 'desert island'.

Fuerteventura is barren and windswept almost to the point of desolation, but it has a grandeur of its own. Craggy mountain ranges, dry *barrancos* (gullies) and cinder-littered *malpaís* typify the harsh terrain.

The wind whistles with great force in Fuerteventura and may even have given the island its name, a corruption and inversion of el *viento fuerte* (the strong wind). However, the constant trade winds have brought good fortune to the island: with the growth of tourism the island has become one of the world's leading windsurfing centres.

The Costa Calma

Parque Natural de Las Dunas de Corralejo

The North

Most people arrive on the island by inter-island ferry to Puerto del Rosario, the capital on the east coast, or at the airport just to the south of the capital, but the once sleepy fishing port of **Corralejo**, at the northern tip, has been transformed into a busy ferry terminal for boats from Lanzarote (it's a 40-minute journey to Playa Blanca). The town has become a bustling resort, and is popular with English visitors. The new developments are not very attractive, but the old harbour area still has colourful fishing boats in it, with some old bars and good fish restaurants lining the quay, and there are the atmospheric back streets to explore. There's not a lot of nightlife, but more than there is in other parts of the island.

The beaches, however, are what people come for and, just outside Corralejo, magnificent, long white beaches and dunes stretch for some 10km (6 miles) down the coast. Although these beaches are a playground, the whole area is protected as the **Parque Natural de Las Dunas de Corralejo**, and inland, where nothing but scrubby succculents grow, you almost feel you could be in the Sahara. Some 3km (2 miles) across a narrow stretch of water, the tiny **Isla de Lobos** is part of the natural park. The beaches are even more secluded here and the fishing is outstanding. Glass-bottomed ferries depart regularly from Corralejo.

There are two routes south to **Puerto del Rosario**, the capital since 1860 and once called Puerto de Cabras (Goat Port) because goats were bred here. The FV-1 follows the east coast, past the dunes, while FV-101 goes inland, where a diversion west will take you to the lace-making town of **Lajares**. At the **Escuela de Artesanía Canaria** (open Mon–Fri 9am–7pm, Sat 9am–3pm; free) you can watch delicate linens being made and embroidered, and buy some.

On the northwest coast lies **El Cotillo**, once a small fishing village with a handful of local bars and restaurants, which is rapidly being developed, owing to the excellent beaches close by that are great for windsurfing.

Back on the main road you reach the little town of **La Oliva**, with old houses the same sandy-ochre shades as the surrounding landscape. The most interesting of the colonial buildings is the **Casa de los Coroneles** (House of the Colonels; Tue–Sat 10am–6pm, www.lacasadeloscoroneles.org), once the home of the 18th-century military governors of the island and now a cultural and exhibition centre after extensive renovation. The building has splendid balconies and exudes a melancholy grandeur. Opposite, in complete contrast, the **Centro de Arte Canario Casa Mane** (open Mon–Fri 10am–5pm, Sat 10am–2pm; http://centrodeartecanario.com) is bright and modern, exhibiting the works of some of the finest contemporary Canarian artists, including Lanzarote's Manrique.

A little further south, just past Tindaya, where the road makes a dog-leg towards Puerto del Rosario, at the foot of the Montaña

Quemada, is the **Monumento de Unamuno**. Writer, philosopher and professor at the University of Salamanca, Unamuno (1864–1936) held staunchly republican views that made him unpopular with the regime of General Primo de Rivera. Exiled to Fuerteventura in 1924, he spent six years here, and often described the beauty of the island in his writing. His most famous quote describes Fuerteventura as 'an oasis in the desert of civilisation.'

During his exile, Unamuno lived in **Puerto del Rosario** in a typical Canarian-style house in Calle Virgen del Rosario. This is now the **Casa Museo Unamuno** (open

Traditional crafts are kept alive in Betancuria

Mon–Fri 9am–2pm, Sat 10am–1pm; free), which is devoted to his life and work.

Even if it has no great architectural merit or other sights of interest, the capital is still worth looking around. The harbour front has been landscaped and smartened up, and there are a few nice old buildings scattered about and some unpretentious restaurants where you can find inexpensive local food. Statues, part of an open-air exhibition, are dotted around the town, adding a cultural slant.

About 10km (6 miles) south of Puerto del Rosario, past the airport, is the cosmopolitan development of **Caleta de Fustes**. Activities here focus on the attractive, horseshoe-shaped beach (where windsurfing is a particularly popular sport) and the well-designed marina. In the marina, there is an area where you can view the fish that frequent its waters and there are a number of boating activities on offer. The circular Castillo de Fustes, from which the resort takes its name, was built in the 18th century, to repel English pirate attacks.

Get back onto the central road, the FV-20, and head for **Antigua**. The architecture of this attractive old town, founded by the early conquerors, shows both Moorish and Spanish influences. It is surrounded by old windmills, which have always had a useful role to play on this windy island.

One of them, set in pleasant cactus gardens, is **El Molino de Antigua**, which has been converted into the **Museo del Queso Majorero** (Majorero Cheese Museum; open Tues–Sat 10am–6pm) and also hosts an exhibition centre dedicated to the local archaeological excavations as well as a handicraft shop.

Follow the road south now, passing the **Mirador de Morro Veloso**, with commanding views of the surrounding mountains and the Atlantic shimmering in the distance, and you will come to **Betancuria**, the most attractive and most visited inland town on Fuerteventura, an oasis of greenery on this otherwise barren island. Although the river bed here is almost perpetually dry, the town is fortunate in having a high water table. Because of its theoretical invulnerability at the heart of the island, it was made Fuerteventura's first capital in the early 15th century. However, in 1539 the ravaging Berber pirates overcame the challenges of the mountain terrain (which still makes a difficult drive today), sacked the town and destroyed the original cathedral.

The present early 17th-century **Iglesia de Santa María** (open Mon–Sat 10am–5pm) is a splendid building, in an eclectic mixture of styles, with painted choir stalls and a decorated wooden ceiling. Lots of gold and silver treasures are kept in the adjacent **Museo de Arte Sacro**. Nearby, in a 16th-century farmhouse,

Punta de Jandía

the Casa Santa María restaurant (www.casasantamaria.net) serves typical local dishes.

Wander around the town and admire the view from across the bridge, where there is a little restaurant and gift shop. On the main street are two interesting museums (both open Tues–Sat 10am–5pm, Sun 11am–2pm), one concentrating on archaeology, the other on traditional crafts. The ruins of a Franciscan convent, the **Ermita de San Diego de Alcalá**, situated to the north of town, are a place of pilgrimage.

Just south of Betancuria is the neat, pretty village of **Pájara**. In a shady square stands the church of the **Virgen de la Regla**, which has a splendid carved stone doorway.

The South

The main southern attractions are the great sandy stretches of beach on the **Jandía Peninsula**, running from the village of Matas Blancas at the narrowest part of Fuerteventura, down to Morro Jable. At the northern tip of the Jandía sands are the beautiful beaches of **Costa Calma**, where the first of the *urbanizaciones* is Canada del Río. There is a great deal of development all along this coast, but some of it is quite well done and there is a low cliff backdrop and a scattering of rocky coves as well as the long stretches of pristine sands.

The **Playa de Sotavento**, some 28km (16 miles) long, is world-famous as a windsurfing beach, with most of the activity focused on the windsurfing school at the Meliá Gorriones Hotel. Here the beach is very wide and flat, protected from the worst of the winds, and, as the tides go out, also very wet. The dunes behind it and a little further to the south form an idyllic beach backdrop.

Urbanizaciones spread relentlessly all the way down the coast to **Morro Jable**, which is a modern port as well as a resort. Ferries go back and forth to Gran Canaria and Tenerife and catamarans take visitors on shorter trips around the coast. The cliffs behind Morro Jable are covered with hotels and apartments, but the resort itself is attractive and bright with shrubs and flowers. There are numerous restaurants, too, as well as miles of wonderful beaches. The area offers everything anyone could wish for in the way of water sports, from windsurfing (of course), kiteboarding and surfing to scuba diving, catamaran sailing and deep-sea fishing.

There are more fine beaches and coves towards the southern tip of the island, such as Playa de Juan Gómez and Playa de las Pilas, but you will need a four-wheel-drive vehicle to get there. Only the brave (or those who go on Jeep safaris, see page 90) get as far as the windswept **Punta de Jandía** and to the wonderfully isolated expanses of sand on the other side of the peninsula – **Playa de Cofete** and **Playa de Barlovento** (Barlovento means windward). Here, only very experienced wind- and kitesurfers take on the elements. Others just soak up the sun, usually in the nude. It's a long way from the real world – but isn't that what a holiday should be?

Island crafts

Fuerteventura is known for its craftwork. Clay is moulded according to ancient techniques into traditional objects such as the *tofio* – a milking bowl – while hats, baskets and brooms are woven out of palm leaves.

WHAT TO DO

ACTIVE PURSUITS

In the fabulously mild climate of the Canaries, most sports are available all year round. Although water sports dominate, there are some surprises – from Canarian wrestling to parachuting.

Water Sports

Scuba Diving. The many firms offering trips and lessons with PADI-qualified divers include: **Gran Canaria**: Centro Turístico de Submarinismo Sun Sub, Playa del Inglés, tel: 928 778 165, www.sunsub.com. **Tenerife**: Calle Maria del Carmen Garcia 22, tel: 922 731 015, www.buceotenerife.com; Los Gigantes Diving Centre, tel: 922 860 431. **Lanzarote**: Island Watersports, Avda. del Varadero 36, 35510 Puerto del Carmen, tel: 928 511 880, www.divelanzarote.com. **Fuerteventura**: Deep Blue Diving, Caleta de Fuste, tel: 928 163 712, www.deep-blue-diving.com. **El Hierro**: Centro de Buceo, La Restinga, tel: 922 557 023, www.centrode buceoelhierro.com.

Windsurfing. The Canaries are a wind- and kitesurfers' delight and **Fuerteventura's** never-ending beaches and cross-shore winds offer perfect conditions March to September. Try the Pro Center René Egli, Sotavento

Safe swimming

Swimming in the sea is relatively safe around all the islands on the designated beaches but currents and waves can develop creating powerful undertows. Look out for a red flag flown when conditions are unsafe for swimming.

Hiking in the Caldera de Taburiente, La Palma

Beach, tel: 928 547 483, www.rene-egli. com; Flag Beach Windsurf Centre, Corralejo, tel: 928 866 389, www.flag-beach.com; check also www.fuerteventura. com/sport. **Gran Canaria**: Dunkerbeck Windsurfing Center, Playa del Águila, San Agustin, tel: 661 052 975, www. dunkerbeck-windsurfing.com; perfect conditions abound in winter at Bahía Feliz, where Club Mistral has a base, tel: 928 157 158/928 774 025. You might also try Ocean-Side Surf Adventures, C./ Almansa, 14 (La Cicer), tel.: 928 220 437: www.ocean-side. eu. **Tenerife**: Surf Center Playa Sur, El Médano, tel: 922 176 688, www.surfcenter.el-medano. com; Fun Factory is based by World Cup beach of El Cabezo, tel: 922 176 273. **Lanzarote**: Windsurf Paradise, Playa de las Cucharas, Costa Teguise, tel: 635 054 110, www.windsurflanzarote.com. All the centres offer tuition at all levels and many do accommodation packages.

Kitesurfing/boarding. Needing similar conditions to windsurfing, kitesurfing tuition and equipment hire are offered by most windsurfing centres (see above). Also try the Kiteboarding School of Fuerteventura, El Cotillo, tel: 928 538 504/678 366 711, www.ksfuerte.com.

Surfing. A few beaches have the right conditions for surfing. Playa de Martiánez in Puerto de la Cruz, **Tenerife** is very popular, as are Playa de las Canteras, in Las Palmas, **Gran Canaria** and La Graciosa, **Lanzarote**. Visit www. surfcanarias.com, www.surflanzarote.com or www.wavepals. com. Tuition and board hire are often offered by windsurfing and kitesurfing centres, as well as accommodation packages (see above).

Sport Fishing. Deep-sea fishing charters for catches including shark, barracuda, marlin and tuna are available at numerous resorts. For example, in **Tenerife**: Los Gigantes, tel: 922 861 918 or http://crestedwave.com; **Gran Canaria**: Puerto Rico, tel: 928 753 013 or www.marlincanariasportfishing.com;

Kitesurfing in Fuerteventura

Lanzarote/Fuerteventura: Puerto del Carmen, tel: 609 886 980, sportfishinglanzarote.com. Lunch is usually included.

Other Activities

Boat and Submarine Trips. Trips from points across the islands, including whale and dolphin safaris and glass-bottomed boats, offer a chance to see marine life without getting wet. **Tenerife/Lanzarote**: Submarine Safaris on both islands offer an hour-long trip in a yellow submarine, when it settles on the seabed, divers feed the fish, tel: 928 512 898 (Lanzarote), 922 736 629 (Tenerife), www.submarine safaris.com. Playa San Juan has *Nostramo*, an original 1918 schooner; Playa de las Américas/Los Cristianos has glass-bottomed boats in Puerto Colón (www.tenerifedolphin. com). **Gran Canaria**: Atlantida Submarine (www.atlantida submarine.com) runs a *Yellow Submarine* in Puerto de Mogán, tel: 928 565 108.

Off-Road Vehicle Adventures. These are very popular in the Canaries where there is plenty of back country rough terrain. **Tenerife**: Quad Bike Safari, Playa de las Américas, tel: 922 714 596; www.tenerife-abc.com/quadbikesafari; Tamarán Jeep Safari, Puerto de Santa Cruz, tel: 922 373 781, and Playa de las Américas, tel: 922 794 757; they also operate in **Lanzarote** at Puerto del Carmen, tel: 928 512 475 www.tamaran.com. **Gran Canaria**: Discovery Jeep Safari, Playa del Inglés, tel: 928 775 188; www.discoverysafari.es. **Fuerteventura**: For Jeep safaris visit www.fuerteventura.com/sport.

Horse Riding. There are reputable stables with instructors at several places across the Canaries. **Tenerife**: Centro Hípico los Brezos, tel: 922 567 222, www.clubhipicolosbrezos.es, near Puerto de la Cruz, with rides over the Tacoronte Hills. **Gran Canaria**: try the horses at Club Hipica Canaria, Calle Secretario Espino, P.I. Maipez, 35220 Jinamar, tel: 670 420

Taking to the saddle at Lanzarote a Caballo

776, www.clubhipicacanaria.com; or Canyon Horse Farm, El Salobre, Maspalomas, tel: 928 143 294.

Ride a Camel. Camel parks and rides are popular on the larger islands. **Gran Canaria:** Camel Safari Park (open daily 9am–6pm), Carretera de Fataga, tel: 928 798 680. **Lanzarote**: Echadero de los Camellos, Montañas del Fuego (open daily 9am–4pm). **Tenerife**: Donkeys can be hired as well as camels at the Camello Center in El Tanque in the northwest, tel: 922 136 191.

Mountain Biking. Bikes can be hired easily at most of the major resorts, where flyers are handed out in the streets. Free-Motion, Playa del Inglés, tel: 928 777 479, www.free-motion. net, hires out mountain bikes.

Skydiving and Hang-Gliding. Gran Canaria: Sky Dive Gran Canaria, Playa del Inglés, tel: 928 157 325 and Paraclub de Gran Canaria, Aeródromo El Berriel, tel: 928 157 000; http://paracaidismograncanaria.com, offer daring visitors the chance to skydive. **Tenerife**: Club Parapente Izana, www.club parapenteizana.com, offers hang-gliding courses.

Walking. All the islands except Fuerteventura and Lanzarote are good for serious walkers. Tourist offices keep a supply of maps of hikes around the islands. **Tenerife**: guided walks and special trails are mapped out for Mount Teide (information from the Parque Nacional del Teide Visitors' Centre – see page 36), and tourist offices will help with trails in other areas; also check www.todotenerife.es. **Gran Canaria**: contact Grupo Montañero Gran Canaria, Las Palmas, tel: 928 427 475, www.gmgrancanaria. com, or the government bookshop, Libería del Cabildo Insular, Calle Cano 24, Las Palmas. **El Hierro**: check with the tourist office in Valverde, tel: 928 550 302 or at: www.trekking-tenerife.com. **Golf**. Most are 18-hole championship standard courses. **Tenerife**: Abama, tel: 922 126 000; www.ritzcarlton.com; Amarilla Golf and Country Club, tel: 922 730 319, www.amarillagolf.es, Golf Las

Américas, tel: 922 752 005, www.golf-tenerife.com and Golf del Sur, tel: 922 738 170, www.golfdelsur.net. **Gran Canaria**: the Real Club de Golf de Las Palmas is on the rim of the Bandama volcanic crater and the oldest in Spain, tel: 928 350 104, www.realclubdegolf delaspalmas.com; for more clubs, visit www.grancanaria golf.org. **Gomera**: La Tecina, tel: 922 145 950; www.jardin-tecina.com. **Lanzarote**: Costa Teguise Golf Club in Tequise, tel: 928 590 512, www.lanzarote-golf. com. **Fuerteventura**: Fuerteventura Golf Resort, tel: 928 160 034; www.fuerteventuragolfclub.com.

SHOPPING

After Spain joined the EU in 1995, the Canary Islands' duty-free status had to change. The islands still retain some tax privileges, but from the visitor's point of view, although there are savings to be made on watches, jewellery and electronic and optical equipment in Las Palmas duty-free shops, there are few real bargains apart from spirits and local tobacco.

Best Buys

In Tenerife, local **wines** are a good thing to take home; buy from the Casa del Vino La Baranda at El Sauzal.

Markets/Mercados

Market are always fun. Prices are flexible and haggling is accepted as part of the process. The biggest, most colourful markets are usually held on Sunday morning. The Sunday morning flea market near the port in Las Palmas is particularly good, and the Mercado de Nuestra Señora de Africa in Santa Cruz de Tenerife (www.la-recova.com) is recommended at any time. Puerto de Mogán, Gran Canaria, has an excellent market by the old port on Friday morning; in Lanzarote, Teguise's Sunday handicaft market is renowned.

Cigars, hand-rolled from locally grown tobacco, are a good buy in La Palma and Tenerife. Among **edible items**, *queso de flor*, the famous cheese made in Guía, Gran Canaria, is a good choice. Jars of *mojo* sauce in many varieties and *bienmesabe* (almond dessert) are widely available. Tenerife honey *(miel)* comes in various guises; the best is from Las Cañadas del Teide. Find out about the different kinds in the Casa de Miel by the Casa del Vino in El Sauzal.

Handicraft items *(artesanía)*, including textiles, baskets and ceramics, can be found in shops and mar-

The market at Teguise, Lanzarote

kets all over Gran Canaria, but the best-quality goods are sold in the outlets of the Federación para la Etnografía y el Desarrollo de la Artesanía Canaria (FEDAC; www.fedac. org). These are situated at Calle Domingo J. Navarro 7, Las Palmas, and in the tourist office in Avenida de España, Playa del Inglés.

In Tenerife, **embroidery** and **lace-making** are traditional, especially tablecloths and cushion covers. Buy from a reputable shop, such as the Casa de los Balcones (www.casa-balcones.com) in La Orotava, or one of its branches. Don't expect bargains; if things are cheap, they are probably mass produced. Artenerife (www.artenerife.com) beside the port in Puerto de la Cruz and Artesanas El Sol in Santa Cruz also specialise in **crafts**.

Last-Minute Special. A few days before you are due to fly home, order some *strelitzias* – Bird of Paradise flowers – or buy them at the airport.

NIGHTLIFE

In the main tourist centres of the Canaries you can find almost any kind of nightlife you want, from extravagant and formal dinner shows to cheap and rowdy karaoke bars, plus clubs and music bars of all kinds. In **Gran Canaria**, Playa del Inglés and Maspalomas are full of them. For serious clubbing head to Kasbah's, The Garage (http://thegarage discopub.com) or Pacha (www.pachagrancanaria.com). The Yumbo Centre is known for its gay bars and clubs, although there are numerous straight venues as well. In Las Palmas, the Mesa y López district is usually the best bet for late-night bars. In **Tenerife**, Playa de las Américas has the most lavish nightlife. Veronicas is the best-known strip, with around 100 bars and clubs that keep going until dawn. Some of the most extravagant shows are at Pirámide de Arona. Tropicana also stages song-and-dance spectaculars. Castillo San Miguel (http://medievaladventure.com), at San Miguel, hosts medieval nights.

Casinos. Gran Canaria: Casino Las Palmas, C/ Simón Bolívar, 3, Las Palmas, tel: 928 234 882; www.casinolas palmas.com; Casino Tamarindos, Retama, 3, tel: 928 762 724, San Agustín. Gran Casino Costa Meloneras, Gran Hotel Costa Meloneras, Maspalomas, tel: 928 14 39 09. **Tenerife**: Casino Puerto de la Cruz, Puerto de la Cruz, tel: 922 36 88 43; Casino Playa de las Américas in the Hotel Gran Tinerfe, Playa de las Américas, tel: 922 79 37 58 and Casino Santa Cruz, tel: 922 82 40 60. You will need your passport to enter the casinos. For more information, check out www.casinos tenerife.com.

FESTIVALS

The folk music of the Canaries is a reminder that the archipelago has always been a bridge between Spain and the New World and much of the music would be equally at home in South America. The Pueblo Canario in Las Palmas is a good place for island song and dance. For a selection of traditional festivals held all over the islands, see page 99.

Carnival

For 10 days each year, usually in mid- to late February, because it precedes Lent, *Carnaval* is the time when thousands of Canarios celebrate in style. Shops and businesses close, and

Traditional costumes and music at a Lanzarote fiesta

young and old flood the streets in fancy dress, dancing to pulsating Latin rhythms. Members of local groups dress according to chosen themes, with magnificent, often outrageous, costumes that can take a whole year to put together. Bands and dancers mingle with elaborate floats. Tourists often don masks and costumes and join in the fun.

Carnaval is biggest and best in Santa Cruz and Puerto de la Cruz in Tenerife and in Las Palmas in Gran Canaria, where it has all the razzmatazz of Rio's *Carnaval* and the Mardi Gras of New Orleans. Hotels are usually full, so book well ahead.

Corpus Christi

Corpus Christi, which can fall any time between the end of May and mid-June, is the most spectacular celebration on the islands after *Carnaval*, although it is of a completely different nature. Coloured volcanic sand, dyed salt or flower petals are painstakingly arranged on paved areas to make up enormous artworks in the form of elaborate abstract patterns or religious pictures, sometimes copied from Old Masters. The most extravagant are

Lucha Canaria and Juego del Palo

Lucha canaria – Canary Islands wrestling – is the most popular traditional sport on the islands and can be seen at rural fiestas and at purpose-built arenas in most Canarian towns. Two teams of 12 wrestlers take it in turns to face a member of the opposing team in a sandy ring, with the aim of throwing the opponent to the ground. After a maximum of three rounds *(bregas)* the winner is the team that loses the fewest wrestlers. The game was practised in pre-Hispanic times, when it may have had more serious overtones.

Juego del Palo (stick fighting) is another ancient rural sport, also practised at fiestas. The object is to move the body as little as possible while attacking and fending off the blows of an opponent.

to be seen in La Orotava and La Laguna in Tenerife, but Las Palmas in Gran Canaria and many other towns and villages in all the islands also participate.

Colourful fiestas of song and dance, food and wine, known as *romerías*, follow hard on the heels of Corpus Christi to redress the balance between sobriety and fun.

Go-karting in Fuerteventura

CHILDREN

With almost guaranteed sunshine, soft sandy beaches, and lots of amusement options on and off the beach, the more popular Canary Islands are perfect for children of all ages. Many hotels have special features for the young, ranging from poolside games and early evening indoor entertainment, to babysitters. Among the other attractions on offer are:

Go-Karting. The go-karts never travel too quickly and are so close to the ground that they don't tip over. Your only problem will be getting your child off when it's time to go. Karting Club Tenerife, Arona (10 minutes from Playa de las Américas) has a normal speed track and a fast track, tel: 922 730 703, www.kartingtenerife.com. Gran Karting Club has a branch in **Gran Canaria**, in Tarajalillo, San Agustín (just off the GC-1 motorway), tel: 928 157 190, and one in **Lanzarote** at La Rinconada (near the airport), both have a fast 'senior track' as well as a child-friendly one, www.grankarting.com.

Museums. Children aren't always enthusiastic about museums, but here are a few that may appeal. **Gran Canaria**: Kids will be fascinated by the Guanche skulls and mummies at the Museo Canario in Las Palmas (see page 61); and the life-size reconstruction of a Guanche settlement at the Mundo Aborigen (open daily 9am–6pm; www.mundo aborigen.es), near Maspalomas; the scientific Museo Elder (Tue–Sun 10am–8pm; www.museoelder.org) in Las Palmas (see page 58) will keep them occupied. **Tenerife**: more Guanche skulls in the Museo de la Naturaleza y el Hombre, Santa Cruz (see page 28); and the Museo de la Ciencia y el Cosmos (open Tue–Sat 9am–8pm, Mon and Sun 10am–5pm; www.museosdetenerife.org), La Laguna, are hands-on for children.

Animal and Bird Parks. **Gran Canaria**: Palmitos Park, close to Playa del Inglés/Maspalomas, has parrots, monkeys, deer, dolphins and crocodiles; (daily 10am–6pm; www.palmitos park.es). **Tenerife**: Loro Parque, Puerto de la Cruz (daily 8.30am–6.45pm; www.loroparque.com), has an aquarium, dolphin and sea lion shows, as well as parrots (see page 30); Parque Las Águilas (open 10am–5.30pm; www.aguilas junglepark.com), at Los Cristianos, has an eagle show, many other birds and animals, and the *Jungle Raid* obstacle course. **Lanzarote**: Lanzarote Aquarium (daily 10am–6pm; www. aquariumlanzarote.com); Las Pardelas Recreational Park (http://pardelas-park.com), at Guinate, has a farm with domestic animals and donkey rides.

Water and Leisure Parks. **Gran Canaria**: Aquasur (open daily 10am–6pm; tel: 928 140 525), near Playa del Inglés, is the Canaries' biggest; Aquapark (open daily 10am–6.30pm in summer and 10am–5.30pm in winter) in Puerto Rico is another winner. **Lanzarote**: Water Park Costa Teguise (http://aquaparklanzarote.es) is the island's best. **Tenerife**: Aqualand (daily 10am–6pm, winter 10am–5pm; www.aqua land.es) in Costa Adeje is a waterpark with a dolphinarium. **Fuerteventura**: Acua Water Park, Corralejo (check www.acua funpark.com for details).

Festival Calendar

6 January: *Cabalgata de los Reyes* (Procession of the Three Kings): costumes, bands, camel cavalcades (Las Palmas, Gran Canaria; Santa Cruz, Garachico, Tenerife; Valle Gran Rey, La Gomera).

February/March: *Carnaval*: several days of fun throughout the islands. *Carnaval de Nuestra Señora del Rosario*: festival of music and dance plus Canarian wrestling (Puerto del Rosario, Lanzarote)

March/April: *Semana Santa*: solemn pre-Easter processions (all islands).

May: *Fiestas de la Cruz*: processions, festivities and fireworks in places with Cruz (cross) in their name.

May/June: *Fiesta de Corpus Christi*: Celebrated in towns and villages everywhere, especially La Laguna and La Orotava (Tenerife), where streets are covered with coloured sand and flowers. Dyed salt is used on the roads of Arrecife (Lanzarote).

July: *Romería de San Benito*: procession of ox-drawn carts (La Laguna, Tenerife). *Fiesta del Mar* (Festival of the Sea): water activities and religious ceremonies combined (Santa Cruz, Puerto de la Cruz, Tenerife).

Fiesta de San Buenaventura: Fuerteventura's islandwide festival featuring Canarian wrestling in Betancuria. *Fiesta de la Virgen del Carmen*: a celebration in all the islands of the patron saint of seamen.

August: *Fiesta de Nuestra Señora de las Nieves*: feast of Our Lady of the Snows (Agaete, Gran Canaria; several locations in La Palma). *Fiesta de la Asunción* (Assumption) reenactment of the appearance of the Virgin to the Guanches (in Candelaria, Tenerife).

September: *Semana de Colón*: Columbus Week (San Sebastián, La Gomera). *Romería de la Virgen del Pino*: religious and secular festivities (Teror, Gran Canaria). *Fiesta de la Virgen de los Volcanes*: celebration of deliverance from volcanic destruction (Mancha Blanca, Lanzarote).

October: *Fiestas de la Naval*: processions in Gran Canarian ports, celebrating the Armada's victory over the English in 1595.

November: *Fiesta del Rancho de Ánimas*: revival of ancient folklore (Teror, Gran Canaria). Kite Festival (Corralejo, Lanzarote).

December: *Fiesta de Santa Lucía*: Feast of Light (Lanzarote; Gran Canaria).

EATING OUT

Canary Islands' food has much in common with that of mainland Spain, but with interesting regional differences. There are also dishes similar to those found in parts of Latin America – although whether these recipes were introduced to the New World by Canarian emigrants, or American inventions brought back by returnees, is debatable.

You will also find many restaurants where the cooking is described as *cocina vasca* (Basque) or *cocina gallega* (Galician). These two regions have a reputation for some of the best cooking in Spain, so they are a welcome addition.

WHERE AND WHEN TO EAT

When it comes to places to eat, the choice is wide. There are some upmarket restaurants in the main towns and resorts that can compete with those in any capital city, and are not expensive by northern European standards. There are fishermen's *tavernas* where the fish is likely to be fresh and wholesome,

Fish in abundance

with few trimmings; and rural *parillas* – grills – where all kinds of meat and sausage are barbecued over an open fire and served with *papas arrugadas* and *mojo rojo* (see page 104).

A *piscolabis* is a snack bar serving a variety of little sandwiches and snacks. When you see restaurants advertising *cocina casalinga* – home-cooking – you'll get

Lunch is served on Playa Blanca's marina, Lanzarote

inexpensive, typically Canarian food, although the quality can vary. There are not many places that style themselves *tapas* bars, but in many middle-of-the-range and inexpensive restaurants there will be a variety of *tapas* on offer, and some of the portions are quite large – two or three would make a meal for most people.

Bars, generally, are places in which to drink, not eat, although most will have croissants or pastries to accompany the morning coffee, some may serve sandwiches (*bocadillos*) or a limited range of *tapas*. A *kiosco* has the same role and these little kiosks can be found in the main squares of most towns and villages.

Meal times are late, as they are on the Spanish mainland; the peak hours are 2–3pm for lunch and around 10pm for dinner. However, restaurants are used to the eating habits of northern Europeans and Americans, and you can get a meal in many places at just about any time of day.

WHAT TO EAT

Fish

As you would expect on an Atlantic island, there is lots of fish and seafood of all kinds. Along with the ubiquitous *sardinas*, fresh from the ocean, the fish most commonly seen on menus are *cherne* (sea bass), *vieja* (parrot fish), *sama* (sea bream) and *bacalao* (salt cod). You will also find *merluza* (hake), *atún* (tuna) and *bonito* (a variety of tuna) and seafood such as *gambas* (prawns), *pulpo* (octopus), *calamares* (squid) and *almejas* (clams).

Often, fish will be served simply grilled along with salad, *mojo* sauce and *papas arrugadas* (see page 104) – a perfectly balanced dish – but there are numerous other ways that it may appear on your table. *Sancocho canario* is a popular dish, a stew made with red grouper or sea bass, potatoes and yams, spiced up with a hot variety of mojo sauce. *Salpicón de pescado* is sea bass or grouper cooked, chopped and served cold with a mixture of onions, garlic, tomatoes and peppers, topped with hard-boiled egg and olives. A delicacy introduced from the

Gofio and its many uses

Made of wheat, barley or a mixture of the two, *gofio* was the staple food of the Guanches and still forms an essential part of the Canarian diet today – you even see sacks of *gofio para perros* (gofio for dogs). The cereal is toasted before being ground into flour which then has a multiplicity of uses. It is stirred into soups and into children's milk and used to thicken sauces. It is made into ice cream and mixed with oil, salt and sugar into a kind of bread, not unlike polenta. It is also sometimes blended with fish stock to make a thick soup called *gofio escaldado*.

Basque country is *calamares rellenos de bacalao* – small squid with a tasty, cod-based stuffing, sometimes served in a creamy sauce.

Paella is not a Canary Island dish, but you can still find it, along with other rice and seafood dishes such as *arroz negro* (rice with squid and squid ink, which makes it black).

Local produce for sale

Meat

The meat menus are extensive, too. *Cabrito* (kid) – sometimes called *baifo* – and *conejo* (rabbit) are most common, along with pork *(cerdo)* and chicken *(pollo)*. There are some good beef steaks to be had in restaurants catering for tourists. Both goat and rabbit are often served *al salmorejo* (with green peppers, in a herb and garlic marinade). *Chorizo* – the red, spicy Spanish sausage, also crops up in a variety of guises.

Soups

Most of the world's traditional dishes originated as a way of filling stomachs with what was available and inexpensive. In the Canary Islands, this meant a whole range of substantial soups and stews. *Ropa vieja* (literally, old clothes) is a mixture of meat, tomatoes and chickpeas; *puchero* includes meat, pumpkin and any vegetables available; while *rancho canari* is the most elaborate and some say the best. Many of the soups contain chunks of corn on the cob. Vegetarians should be aware that even watercress soup *(potaje de berros)*, a staple of many menus, has chunks of bacon in it. And celery soup *(potaje de apio)* may contain scraps of pork.

Vegetables

The vegetables you are offered will be those that are in season and because the island does not produce a great variety, and imports are expensive, choice may be limited. Pulses such as lentils (*lentejas*) and chickpeas (*garbanzos*) are used a lot; Canary tomatoes are delicious. If you like garlic, ask for *tomates aliñados*, tomato salad smothered with olive oil and garlic. *Pimientos de padrón* – small green peppers cooked whole and covered with salt – originated in Galicia and are now found everywhere. Avocados (strictly speaking a fruit not a vegetable) are served perfectly ripe.

Most dishes contain or are accompanied by potatoes (*papas*), and sometimes by *ñame*, a kind of yam. You'll encounter *papas arrugadas* (wrinkled potatoes), which are served with meat and fish or as *tapas*. They are small potatoes – the yellow-fleshed Tenerife variety are best – cooked in their skins in salted water then dried over a low heat until their skins wrinkle and a salty crust forms. It is said that this dish originated with fishermen who used to boil the potatoes in seawater.

Mojo

Papas arrugadas, and many meat dishes, are usually accompanied by *mojo rojo*, a sauce whose basic ingredients are tomatoes, peppers and paprika. A spicier version (*mojo picón*) contains hot chilli as well. *Mojo verde* is a green sauce made with oil, vinegar, garlic, coriander and parsley, usually served with fish. The sauces arrive at the table in small bowls so you can use as much or as little as you like.

Cheese, Fruit and Desserts

There are only a few Canary Island cheeses, but they are delicious. The best known is an award-winning soft cheese, *queso de flor*, made in Guía, Gran Canaria, using a mixture of sheep's and cows' milk curdled with the juice of flowers from the cardoon thistle. Another award-winner, *queso tierno de Valsequillo*, is a mild,

Papas arrugadas with mojo rojo

smooth cheese like mozzarella. Fuerteventura is known for its award-winning goat's cheese, *Majorero*. The young, fresh cheese has a white rind and a crumbly texture; the matured version has a yellow rind, which may be rubbed with oil or paprika or, sometimes, *gofio*. You will find it on most menus in Fuerteventura, and quite a few on Lanzarote.

Home-grown Canary Island fruit is delicious. As well as the small, local bananas, there are papayas, guavas, mangoes and oranges, delicious by themselves, made into juice or used to flavour ice cream. On many menus desserts are limited to ice cream *(helado)*, *flan* (caramel custard), fresh fruit, and the one you see everywhere, *bienmesabe*, which translates as 'tastes good to me' – and so it does. There are many recipes, but basically it is a mixture of crushed almonds, lemon, sugar (lots), cinnamon and egg yolks. El Hierro is noted for its *quesadilla*, a fluffy cake made with lemon and cheese.

Alcoholic Drinks

A Glass of Sack

In Shakespeare's day sherry wine was called 'sack' or 'sherries sack'. 'Sack' derived from the Spanish word *sacar* (to export), while 'sherries' comes from the name of the town Jerez, where this wine originated.

In Elizabethan times, Canaries wine was served at all the top tables in Europe. Tastes may have changed, but the local wines are still very good. Unfair as it may seem, local wines are dearer than table wines imported from the mainland because they are made on a much smaller scale.

Several of the vines flourish because of the volcanic soil, giving the wine a rich, full flavour. Historically, Canaries wines were of the Malmsey (*malvasía*) variety. These tend to be very sweet, but there are drier varieties that retain the same rich, distinctive bouquet. You are more likely to be offered local wines in country restaurants than in the big resorts.

Rum (*ron*) is made in the Canaries and is very popular. It is often mixed with Coca-Cola in a *Cuba libre*. The liqueur *ronmiel* (literally, rum honey) is a La Gomera speciality.

Local distilleries also produce fruit-based liqueurs; particularly banana, but also orange and other tropical flavours.

Sangría is a popular tourist drink throughout Spain. It is a mixture of red wine, orange and lemon juices, brandy and mineral water topped with lots of sliced fruit and ice.

Sherry (*jerez*), that most famous of Spanish drinks, is not as popular in the Canaries as it is on the mainland, but with Spanish brandy (colloquially known as *coñac*) and Spanish-style champagne (*cava*), it is available in good bars and served in huge measures.

Supermarket shelves are full of the same names at eye-poppingly low prices and are much cheaper than airport duty-free shops. Canarian beer (*cerveza*) is usually Tropical or the well-recommended Dorada lager. Beer is served either draught or in bottles measuring one-third of a litre. Draught measures vary but if you want a small beer ask for *una cerveza pequeña*, or *una caña*.

Una cerveza grande can vary in size, but is often around a pint. Remember that Spanish lager is a bit stronger than some of the lagers popular in the UK and most US beers.

Tea, Coffee and Soft Drinks

The Spanish usually drink coffee *(café)* rather than tea *(té)*. This can be either solo (small and black), *con leche* (a large cup made with milk, often in a frothy cappuccino-style), or *cortado* (a small cup with a little milk). Mineral water *(agua mineral)* is either sparkling *(agua con gas)* or still *(agua sin gas)*. Ice-cream parlours sell *granizado*, slushy iced fruit juice in various flavours, and freshly pressed orange juice *(zumo de naranja)*, the latter being surprisingly expensive.

At bodegas you can try wine from the barrel before buying

TO HELP YOU ORDER

Could we have a table? **¿Nos puede dar una mesa, por favor?**

Do you have a set menu? **¿Tiene un menú del día?**

I would like... **Quisiera...**

The bill, please **La cuenta, por favor**

DECIPHERING THE MENU

agua minerale mineral water

à la plancha grilled

al ajillo in garlic

al punto medium

arroz rice

asado roast

atún tuna

azúcar sugar

bacalao cod

bocadillo sandwich

boquerones anchovies

bien hecho well done

buey/res beef

café coffee

calamares squid

callos tripe

cangrejo crab

cerdo pork

cerveza beer

champiñones mushrooms

chorizo spicy sausage

cocido stew

cordero lamb

ensalada salad

entremeses hors-d'oeuvre

flan caramel custard

helado ice cream

jamón serrano cured ham

judías beans

langosta lobster

leche milk

mariscos shellfish

mejillones mussels

morcilla black pudding

pan bread

pescado fish

picante spicy

poco hecho rare

pollo chicken

postre dessert

puerco pork

pulpitos baby octopus

queso cheese

sal salt

ternera veal

tortilla omelette

trucha trout

salsa sauce

vino wine

verduras vegetables

PLACES TO EAT

This is just a small selection of the many excellent restaurants on the islands. The following categories indicate the approximate price per person for a three-course meal including half a bottle of house wine (restaurants are listed alphabetically within islands, not within towns):

€€€ 35–50 euros   **€€** 20–35 euros   **€** below 20 euros

TENERIFE

Anturium in Hotel San Roque €€€ *Calle Esteban de Ponte 32, Garachico, tel: 922 133 435*, http://hotelsanroque.com. The cuisine is a mix of Canarian and Mediterranean cuisines with delicacies such as *dorada en sal* (bream baked in rock salt) and *paella duo* (with squid). Great selection of wines.

Arepera Punto Criollo € *Calle El Tizón, 6, San Cristobal de la Laguna, tel: 922 257 007.* One of the best traditional restaurants famous for its *gofio* and *arepas* (Venezuelan flatbread) with different fillings. Perfect location in the old part of La Laguna.

Café del Principe €€ *Plaza del Principe del Asturias, Santa Cruz, tel: 922 278 810.* This iron-and-glass Art Nouveau pavilion set in a shady town square is an enjoyable place for tapas of *pulpo con mojo* or a full meal.

El Drago €€€ *Carrer Marqués de Celada 2, Tegueste, tel: 922 543 001*, www.mesoneldrago.com. This family-run award-winning establishment serves some of the best Canarian dishes on Tenerife, much of which are their own creations, such as watercress soup with yams and red onion, cheese and *gofio*. Special menu for kids.

Gastrobar MNH Armando Saldanha €€ *Calle Fuente Morales s/n, Santa Cruz, tel: 922 083 043*, www.museosdetenerife. org. A small cafeteria in the Museo de la Naturaleza y El Hombre opened by the acclaimed Mexican chef Armando Saldanha, who is famous for his *tapas*.

El Gusto por el Vino € *Av. San Sebastían 51, Mercado La Recova, Santa Cruz,* www.elgustoporelvino.com. A restaurant and a wine-bar run by the biggest local wine distributor in the popular La Recova market. Short but tasty menu of tapas.

La Posada del Pez €€ *Carretera Taganana 2, San Andrés, tel: 922 591 948.* A small but excellent seafood restaurant near the Playa de las Teresitas. The dish *A mar y montaña* (sea and montain), a mix of fish and oxtail all in one plate, is worth a try. Sunday closed for dinner.

Régulo €€€ *Calle Pérez Zamora 16, Puerto de la Cruz, tel: 922 384 506,* www.restauranteregulo.com. Excellent food served in a typical 18th-century Canarian house with ornate balconies and a central patio. Specialities include grilled limpets and *solomillo relleno de camembert* (steak with camembert). Open for lunch and dinner, closed Sunday, Monday lunch and for the month of July.

El Rincón de Juan Carlos €€€ *Pasaje de Jacaranda 2, Los Gigantes, tel: 922 868 040,* www.elrincondejuancarlos.es. A romantic family restaurant located on a quiet street with a lovely terrace. Exquisite signature dishes. Closed Sundays.

Sabor Canario €€ *Carrera Escultor Estevez, 17, La Orotava, tel: 922 322 793,* http://hotelruralorotava.es. In a 16th-century townhouse, serving traditional dishes, including rabbit in *solmerejo* sauce, and *gofio*.

El Sol chez Jacques €€€ *Paseo Roma s/n, Los Cristianos, tel: 922 790 569.* Opened in 1974 it's one of the oldest restaurants on the island, serving classic French fare, including a superb beef Bourguignon with six homemade sauces. Open for dinner only, closed Mondays in May and the whole of June.

La Tasca €€€ *Gran Hotel Bahia del Duque, Avenida Bruselas s/n, Playa de las Américas, tel: 922 746 932,* www.bahia-duque.com. Spanish in decor, style and cuisine, with staff in traditional costumes. Good place to taste typical Spanish staples.

La Vará del Puerto €€ *Calle Albareda 89, Las Palmas, tel: 667 284 683*. This new self-service seafood restaurant offers a real feast for just €15 or €20, wine included. Great selection of seafood, which is served steamed, fried or grilled with *mojo verde* or *mojo rojo*. Closed Monday and Tuesday.

EL HIERRO

Mirador de la Peña €€ *Ctra General del Norte 40, Guarazoca, tel: 922 550 300*. A *mirador* restaurant designed by local artist César Manrique. Island specialities are served in a contemporary decor with wonderful views. Closed Monday.

LA GOMERA

Club Laurel €€€ *Lomada de Tecina, Playa de Santiago, tel: 922 145 850, www.jardin-tecina.com*. Part of the Hotel Jardín Tecina, this restaurant by the beach serves *haute cuisine* and has an evening smart dress code policy. Closed Mon, Thu and Sat.

Mirador César Manrique €€€ *tra General de Arure, Valle Gran Rey, tel: 922 805 868*. This restaurant enjoys a dramatic position overlooking the mountains and a beautiful garden. Excellent meat dishes and good service.

Las Rosas € *Ctra General, Las Rosas, tel: 922 800 916, www.fredolsen. es*. This Las Rosas serves up Gomeran cuisine in a setting of panoramic views of Tenerife and Mount Teide. When coach parties arrive, demonstrations of *el silbo*, the island's whistling language, are given. Lunch only.

LA PALMA

Las Goteras € *Parque Recreativo de La Laguna de Barlovento, tel: 922 696 456, http://lasgoteras.com*. Set in a beautiful, serene garden. Try the delicious grilled cheese with *mojo* sauce. Closed Monday.

El Jardin de la Sal €€ *Carretera el Faro, 5, tel: 922 979 800, http:// salinasdefuencaliente.es*. This beautifully located restaurant specialising in local cuisine offers the freshest seafood and endless views over the Atlantic Ocean.

Parador de la Palma €€€ *El Zumacal, Breña Baja, tel: 922 435 828,* www.parador.es. Traditional dishes including *conejo en mojo hervido* (rabbit in a *mojo* sauce) are served in an attractive dining room or on a terrace.

La Placeta €€ *Placeta Borrero 1, Santa Cruz, tel: 922 415 273,* www. restaurantelaplaceta.com. This restaurant, set in an attractive old house, has a delightful atmosphere. The food is home cooked, with an emphasis on fish and meat in a variety of sauces. Closed Sunday.

GRAN CANARIA

La Casa Vieja € *Carretera de Fataga 139, Maspalomas, tel: 928 769 010.* Barbecued meat and goat stews served in an old country house with rustic decor, but only a short taxi ride from the tourist centres.

Deliciosa Marta €€ *Perez Galdos 23, Las Palmas, tel: 928 370 882.* Arguably the best restaurant of Las Palmas: good food, friendly staff and lovely romantic ambience. The lamb shoulder and steak tartare are recommended. Advance booking is essential.

El Herreño €€ *Calle Medizábal 5, Las Palmas, tel: 928 310 513.* Situated close to the Vegueta market, this restaurant is a Las Palmas institution. It serves hearty, simple food from El Hierro in a relaxed and friendly atmosphere. Large families sit at long tables to enjoy thick seafood stews followed by *gofio* mousse and *bienmesabe*. Plenty of vegetarian options.

La Marinera €€ *Paseo de Las Canteras la Puntilla, Las Palmas, tel: 928 461 555/928 468 022,* www.restaurantelamarineralaspalmas. com. At the end of Playa de las Canteras, this restaurant has a dining room so close to the sea that you could almost catch the fish yourself. Fortunately, they do it for you, and cook it extremely well.

Mesón La Cilla € *Camino la Cilla 9, tel: 928 666 108.* This is the famous cave restaurant, with spectacular views from its sunny terrace, and kitchens cut into the rock. It serves typical, robust meat dishes, many with *mojo* sauce. Closes at sunset.

Qué tal by Stena €€ *Puerto de Mogán, tel: 928 56 55 34*, http://quetalbystena.com. The concept here is a short, five-course set menu and some of the dishes are prepared in front of customers. Great atmosphere. Open for dinner only.

Racimo 16 € *Lucas Fernández Navarro, 55, Las Palmas, tel: 673 242 002*. This simple cafeteria offers a short menu based on daily organic products. There is always a fish, meat and vegetarian dish to choose from. Ideal for lunch, a set menu costs only €10.

Ribera del Río Miño €€€ *Calle Olof Palme, 21, Las Palmas, tel: 928 264 431*. Despite being expensive, this smart restaurant close to Playa de las Canteras and Plaza España has quickly become very popular. Recommended for its Galician cuisine and good wines.

Samsara €€ *Avenida del Oasis 30, Maspalomas, tel: 928 142 736*, www.samsara-gc.com. This Asian restaurant is a good place for a romantic evening. The menu is mostly Asian fusion and the carpaccios of tuna or duck are delicious. Book in advance.

Tenderete II €€, *Edificio Aloe 3, Avenida de Tirajana 15, Playa del Inglés, tel: 928 767 180*, http://restaurantetenderete.com. On the ground floor of an apartment block, this doesn't look much from the outside, but the food inside has been consistently good for years. Do try the *rancho canario* (a thick wholesome meaty Spanish soup).

LANZAROTE

Caserio de Mogaza €€ *Mogaza, tel: 928 520 060*, http://caseriodemozaga.com. The restaurant in this *casa rural* is one of the best places to eat on the island. Excellent fresh local ingredients are used in the dishes, and it's difficult to choose between the wonderful desserts, all served in the attractive setting of a converted barn.

La Era €€€ *Yaiza, tel: 928 830 016*, www.laera.com. This well-known restaurant serves outstanding island food in a 300-year-old Canarian farmhouse with a whitewashed courtyard. There is also an art-filled, wooden-beamed bar that serves snacks and light meals. Yet another César Manrique creation.

Jardín de Cactus €€ *Guatiza, tel: 928 529 397*, www.centro sturisticos.com. Good, simple Canarian lunches are served on a shady terrace overlooking the beautiful cactus garden designed by César Manrique. The homemade *gofio* is recommended. Lunch only.

La Lonja €€ *Calle Varadero s/n, Puerto del Carmen, tel: 928 511 377*. This two-part establishment has a wonderful *tapas* bar and fresh fish shop on the ground floor and a restaurant serving the very best grilled fish and shellfish on the second. Open daily.

Mesón La Jordana €€ *Calle Los Geranios s/n, Costa Teguise, tel: 928 590 328*. Popular, long-established restaurant just two minutes from Lanzarote Bay Hotel. Serves up local favourites such as rabbit, kid and lamb, as well as international dishes. Closed Sunday.

Qué Muac €€ *Castillo de San José, Arrecife, tel: 928 812 321*, www. centrosturisticos.com.This restaurant is set in the castle housing the Contemporary Art Museum. On the menu: a great selection of *tapas* and some tasty fish and meat dishes based on local products, plus sweeping vistas over the sea.

FUERTEVENTURA

Casa Princess Arminda €€ *Calle Juan de Betancort 2, Betancuria, tel: 638 802 780*, www.princessarminda.com. This bar and restaurant is set in a house owned by the same family for the last 500 years. The bar, dining room and pretty courtyard make for a pleasant setting to sample the dishes prepared with local. Be tempted by the excellent goat stew.

Punta Dell'Este €€ *Calle Hermanas del Castillo 4, El Cotillo, tel: 928 538 483*. A popular Italian restaurant with mountain views and friendly staff. The seafood pasta, homemade bread and coffee are excellent.

A–Z TRAVEL TIPS

A Summary of Practical Information

A

ACCOMMODATION

Most accommodation in the Canaries is designed for family package holidays and tends to be of a medium-high international standard. There are also apartments and 'aparthotels', where each room has its own kitchen facilities yet retains all the trappings of a hotel. If you plan to visit during the high seasons (late Nov–Mar and July–Aug), book accommodation well in advance through a travel agent or directly with the hotel. For a comprehensive listing of accommodation and rates throughout Spain, consult the *Guía Oficial de Hoteles*– available from The Spanish National Tourist Office (see page 131). Breakfast is not always included, so check when you book.

It's not easy to find cheap accommodation in the major resorts if you are travelling independently, with the majority of places being at least 3- or 4-star hotels. However, the large towns, such as Santa Cruz and Las Palmas, will have a selection of lower-rated places.

There is a growing number of *casas rurales* – rural properties or old town houses that have been converted into small hotels or renovated and rented as self-catering accommodation. For information go to www.ecoturismocanarias.com.

Paradors are state-run hotels, often housed in historic buildings outside towns and in rural areas. There are *paradores* in Tenerife, El Hierro, Fuerteventura and La Palma. Advance booking is highly recommended. Contact Paradores de Turismo, Central de Reservas, Requena 3, 28013 Madrid, tel: 91 516 67 00; www.paradores-spain.com or www.parador.es.

---

a single/double room **una habitación sencilla/doble**
with bath and toilet/shower **con baño/ducha**
What's the rate per night? **Cuál es el precio por noche?**

AIRPORTS

All the islands have commercial airports.

Tenerife: Reina Sofia (Tenerife Sur), tel: 902 404 704; Los Rodeos (Tenerife Norte), tel: 902 404 704/922 553 700
La Palma: tel: 902 404 704/91 321 10 00
El Hierro: tel: 902 404 704
La Gomera: tel: 902 404 704
Gran Canaria: Aeropuerto de Gando, tel: 902 404 704
Lanzarote: tel: 902 404 704.
Fuerteventura: tel: 902 404 704.

All the airports are served by taxis and the major airports also have regular bus services. Car-hire companies have outlets in the arrivals terminals. Visitors on package holidays will be met at the airport by coaches and tour company representatives. For general information see www.aena.es.

B

BUDGETING FOR YOUR TRIP

To give you an idea of what to expect, here's a list of some average prices in euros. They can only be approximate, as prices vary from place to place, and inflation in Spain, as elsewhere, creeps up relentlessly.

Accommodation. Rates for two sharing a double room can range from as low as €30 at a *pensión* or *hostal* to as much as €360–420 at a top-of-the-range five-star hotel. A pleasant three-star will cost around €90. Rates drop considerably out of season – May to June and September to October.

Attractions. Most museums and gardens charge a small entry fee of around €4–5. The larger attractions, where you might spend a day, charge between €10 and €30; children are often half price.

Car rental. Including comprehensive insurance and tax, rates are around €35 a day from the big international companies; you get a better deal if you book for a week. Cars booked in advance via the internet may also be considerably cheaper.

Getting there. Air fares vary enormously, with those from the UK to Gran Canaria or Tenerife ranging between £150 and £400 (€210–565). As with hotels, you will get the best deals in May to June and September to October. From the US, flights cost around $980.

Meals and drinks. In a bar a continental breakfast will cost around €4–5. The cheapest three-course set meal *(menú del día)*, including one drink, will be around €8. The average price of a three-course, à-la-carte meal, including house wine, will be about €25 per person, and twice as much in a top restaurant.

Petrol. Very cheap by UK standards – around €0.90 a litre.

Taxis. Prices are controlled and reasonable. In Gran Canaria, for example, the fare from Gando airport to Las Palmas is around €23. In Tenerife, from Reina Sofía airport to Playa de Las Américas, around €18. Trips within cities don't cost more than about €4.

C

CAR HIRE (See also Driving)

Normally you must be over 21 to rent a car, and you will need a valid driver's licence that you have held for at least 24 months, your passport, and a major credit card to serve as deposit. Automatic cars are available, but not many and are usually more expensive. All the big international companies have offices at the

I'd like to rent a car for one day/week. **Quisiera alquilar un coche por un día/una semana.**
Please include full insurance. **Haga el favor de incluir el seguro a todo riesgo.**

airports and in the major cities and there are numerous local companies. **CICAR (Canary Islands Car)**, tel: 928 822 900, www.cicar.com, has been in business for over 30 years and has outlets on each island. Their offices are easily recognisable by the modern, colourful, logo designed by César Manrique. **Auto Reisen** (www.arcarhire.com) also has outlets on the four larger islands. You can usually pick up and drop off your car at the airport.

CLIMATE

Despite the popular concept that sunshine is guaranteed here, it is impossible to generalise about the islands. It may be pouring with chilly rain on La Gomera or La Palma, while sunbathers bake on Fuerteventura. The mountainous nature of Gran Canaria and the north–south divide of Tenerife mean that the weather can be completely different at opposite ends of each island.

There are two rules of thumb: the easterly islands are drier and warmer than the westerly ones (Lanzarote and Fuerteventura are normally a little warmer than Gran Canaria); the sunnier, warmer weather is likely to be found on the south side of an island.

Be prepared for winds: in spring there is a cold and wet gust from the northwest, and in autumn the famous sirocco.

Approximate monthly average temperature:

	J	F	M	A	M	J	J	A	S	O	N	D
°C	17	16	17	18	21	22	23	24	23	22	20	18
°F	64	62	64	64	68	71	74	75	74	70	69	64

CLOTHING

In addition to summer clothes and beachwear, don't forget a sweater or jacket for cooler evenings and air-conditioned shops and restaurants. For excursions to high altitudes you will need warmer clothing and some sturdy shoes. In winter, waterproofs may be needed.

Casual wear is the norm, although in five-star hotels, the best restaurants and casinos, a jacket and tie for men is preferred.

Topless bathing is acceptable at most hotel pools. Don't offend local sensibilities by wearing shorts, bikini tops or anything too revealing in city streets, or when visiting churches and museums.

CRIME

The most common crime against tourists in the Canaries is theft from hired cars. Never leave anything of value in your car. Use the safe deposit box in your room for all valuables, including your passport (carry a photocopy with you). Keep apartment doors and windows locked when you are absent and while you are asleep. However, the Canaries do not have a high crime rate, so just take the usual sensible precautions. You must report all thefts to the local police within 24 hours for your own insurance purposes.

I want to report a theft. **Quiero denunciar un robo.**

CUSTOMS AND ENTRY FORMALITIES

Most visitors, including citizens of all EU countries, the US, Canada, Ireland, Australia and New Zealand, require only a valid passport to enter Spain and the Canary Islands. Visitors from South Africa must have a visa. If in doubt, contact the Spanish consulate in your home country before leaving.

Although Spain is in the EU there is still a restriction on duty-free allowances at customs (*aduana*) when returning to the UK from the Canary Islands. This is 200 cigarettes or 50 cigars or 250g smoking tobacco; 1 litre spirits over 22 percent or 2 litres under 22 percent, and 2 litres of wine.

Currency restrictions. Tourists may bring an unlimited amount of euros or foreign currency into the country.

D

DRIVING

Driving conditions. The rules are the same as in mainland Spain and the rest of the European continent: drive on the right, pass on the left, yield right of way to all vehicles coming from your right. Speed limits are 120km/h (74mph) on motorways, 100km/h (62mph) on dual highways, and 50km/h (31mph) in built-up areas and 20km/h (13mph) in residential areas.

Roads vary from a six-lane highway (in Santa Cruz de Tenerife) and a new motorway system around Las Palmas de Gran Canaria, to primitive tracks in rural areas. In every main city, and even in smaller provincial ones, traffic can be appalling and one-way systems confusing. Do not drive unless you have to in these towns.

There are many narrow mountain roads, where you'll need to use your horn at every bend. At any time you may come across a herd of goats, a donkey and cart, a large pothole, or rocks falling as you round the next bend. Always slow down when passing through villages. Allow more time than you think a journey will take from simply looking at the map. Driving on mountain roads all day can be very tiring, so take frequent breaks.

Parking. It is almost impossible to park in the capitals and other large towns. It is an offence to park facing against the traffic.

Petrol. Petrol is much cheaper than in the UK and the rest of Europe. Unleaded petrol is called *sin plomo*. Some larger petrol stations are open 24 hours and most accept credit cards. In rural areas there are very few petrol stations.

Traffic police. Armed civil guards *(Guardia Civil)* patrol the roads on black motorcycles. In towns, the municipal police handle traffic control. If you are fined for a traffic offence, you must pay on the spot.

Rules and regulations. Always carry your driving licence with you. It is a good idea to have a photocopy of the important pages of your passport. If you are driving your own car, your insurance company will provide you with a green card and bail bond, which you need for driving in Spain. If you have a hire car, insurance documents will be provided by the rental firm. Seat belts are compulsory everywhere. Children under 10 must travel in the rear. Using mobile phones or GPS devices while moving is illegal.

Road signs. Aside from the standard pictographs you may see:

Aparcamiento Parking
Desviación Detour
Obras Road works
Peatones Pedestrians
Peligro Danger
Salida de camiones Truck/lorry exit

Or you may need to say:

¿Se puede aparcar aquí? Can I park here?
Llénelo, por favor, con super. Fill the tank please, top grade.
Ha habido un accidente. There has been an accident.

E

ELECTRICITY

220 volts is now standard, but older installations of 125 volts can occasionally be found. An adaptor for continental-style two-pin sockets will be needed and American 110V appliances need a transformer.

EMBASSIES AND CONSULATES

Province of Santa Cruz de Tenerife
UK: Plaza Weyler 8, 1º, Santa Cruz de Tenerife, tel: 902 109 356.
US: Calle Martínez Escobar 3, Oficina 7, Las Palmas de Gran Ca-

naria, tel: 928 271 259.
Ireland: Calle San Francisco, 1º, tel: 922 245 671.
Province of Las Palmas de Gran Canaria
UK: Calle Luís Morote 6, Las Palmas, tel: 928 262 508.
US: Calle Martínez Escobar 3, Oficina 7, Las Palmas, tel: 928 271 259.
Ireland: Calle León y Castillo 195, Las Palmas, tel: 928 297 728.

Where is the American/ British consulate? **¿Dónde está el consulado americano/británico?**

EMERGENCIES

The emergency numbers are common to all the Canary Islands.
General emergencies: 112
Police: 091
Local police: 092
Guardia Civil: 062
Ambulance: 061
Fire Brigade: 080

G

GAY AND LESBIAN TRAVELLERS

Major resorts in the Canary Islands have developed facilities for gay and lesbian travellers, including dedicated hotels. Visit www.thegay canaries.com or www.gcgay.com for details. In Playa del Inglés, Gran Canaria, the Yumbo Centre has lots of gay bars, restaurants and clubs.

GETTING THERE

By air. See also Airports. There are numerous scheduled and budget airline flights from all UK airports to Tenerife and Gran Canaria. There are some direct flights to Lanzarote, with British Airways, but most Iberia and other flights involve a stop-over in Madrid or Barcelona. Otherwise fly to Gran Canaria or Tenerife and get a connecting flight. The direct flight time is four to four-and-a-half hours. Check the web and advertisements in the travel sections of Sunday papers for good flight-only deals. Many people go to the Canaries on all-in package holidays, which can be the cheapest way to do it. For Iberia, the Spanish national carrier, tel: 02 036 843 774, www.iberiaairlines.co.uk; British Airways, tel: 0844 493 0787, www.britishairways.com; Norwegian, www.norwegian.com

For the smaller islands, travel to Las Palmas or Tenerife then take an inter-island flight, run by Binter Airlines, tel: 902 391 392/928 579 433, www.bintercanarias.es.

At present there are several direct flights from the islands the US (New York, Los Angeles, Chicago) operated by British Airways, Iberia, Norwegian, Condor and Lufthansa. Indirect flights go via Madrid or Barcelona, or via London airports; check with a travel agency, or visit www.opodo.com.

By ship: The Trasmediterránea ferry company runs a weekly service from Cádiz to Arrecife, Las Palmas, Santa Cruz de Tenerife, Santa Cruz de la Palma, which takes around 48 hours. For details, tel: 902 454 645, or visit www.trasmediterranea.es. Trasmediterránea operates jetfoils between Tenerife, Gran Canaria and Fuerteventura, and runs ferries to all the islands except La Gomera and El Hierro.

The Fred Olsen Shipping Line (tel: 902 100 107/928 495 040/922 628 200, www.fredolsen.es) runs ferries between Gran Canaria and Tenerife six times a day from Puerto de las Nieves, Agaete (journey time about 70 minutes; free bus from Las Palmas); and between Tenerife and El Hierro (journey time 2 hours). Naviera Armas (tel: 902 456 500, www.naviera-armas.com) has services from Gran Canaria to Tenerife, Fuerteventura and Lanzarote, and Tenerife to El Hierro and La Palma.

GUIDES AND TOURS

All the major islands are comprehensively covered by tour operators, whose coaches take tourists everywhere that is worth seeing. They all have local offices but can also be booked through hotels.

H

HEALTH AND MEDICAL CARE

Anything other than basic emergency treatment can be very expensive, and you should not leave home without adequate insurance, including coverage for an emergency flight home in the event of serious injury or illness.

The EHIC card, which entitles EU citizens to free health care, is available in the UK from post offices or online at www.ehic.org.uk. Before being treated it is advisable to check that the doctor is working within the Spanish Health Service. You will probably have to pay for the treatment or medicines and claim a refund when you get back home, so keep receipts.

Pharmacies (Farmacias). Pharmacies are usually open during normal shopping hours. After hours, at least one per town, called *farmacia de guardia*, remains open all night and its location is posted in the window of all other *farmacias* and in the newspapers.

Where's the nearest (all-night) chemist? **¿Dónde está la farmacia (de guardia) más cercana?**
I need a doctor/dentist. **Necesito un médico/dentista.**
sunburn/sunstroke **quemadura del sol/una insolación**
an upset stomach **molestias de estómago**

L

LANGUAGE

The Spanish spoken in the Canary Islands is slightly different from that of the mainland. For instance, islanders don't lisp when they pronounce the letters *c* or *z*. The language of the Canaries is spoken with a slight lilt, reminiscent of parts of Latin America. A number of New World words and expressions are used. The most commonly heard are *guagua* (pronounced *wah-wah*), meaning bus, and *papa* (potato). In tourist areas basic German, English and some French is often spoken, or at least understood.

The *Berlitz Spanish Phrasebook and Dictionary* covers most situations you may encounter in Spain and the Canaries.

> Do you speak English? **¿Habla usted inglés?**
> I don't speak Spanish. **No hablo español.**

M

MEDIA

Radio and television (*radio, televisión*). Many hotels have satellite TV with copious channels in various languages, including CNN. The larger islands all include some English-language news and tourist information in their programming. TV Canarias is a local station dedicated to the attractions of the islands. English-language radio stations include Atlantis FM 98.2 MHz; Power FM 98.2 MHz; UK Away FM 99.9 MHz (Lanzarote).

Newspapers and periodicals. Many British and Continental newspapers are on sale in the major resorts and in Santa Cruz de Tenerife and Las Palmas on the day of publication, as is the European edition of the *New York Herald Tribune*. There are a number of English-language publications with island news and tourist information (mostly free), but are not evenly distributed. They include *Holiday Gazette & Tourist Guide* (monthly; http://thegazettelive. com), *Island Connections* www.ic-web.com, and various property-based publications.

There is a good annual restaurant and hotel guide called *¡Qué Bueno!* (separate publications for Tenerife and Gran Canaria), which are in both English and Spanish.

For Spanish speakers, the island newspapers are *Canarias7* and *La*

Provincia: *Diario de Las Palmas*. They have listings of events so can be useful even if your Spanish is very sketchy.

MONEY

Currency. The monetary unit in the Canary Islands, as throughout Spain, is the euro, which is abbreviated to €.

Bank notes are available in denominations of €500, 200, 100, 50, 20, 10 and 5. The Euro is subdivided into 100 cents, and there are coins available for €1 and €2 and for 50, 20, 10, 5, 2 and 1 cents.

Currency exchange. Banks are the best place to exchange currency, but *casas de cambio* exchange foreign currency and stay open outside banking hours, as do many businesses displaying a *cambio* sign. All larger hotels will also change guests' money, but the rates they offer will be slightly less than at a bank. Both banks and exchange offices pay slightly less for cash than for travellers cheques. Remember to take your passport with you when you go to change money. Or use a cash machine for the best exchange rate.

Credit cards. Most international cards are widely recognised, although smaller businesses tend to prefer cash. Visa/Eurocard/MasterCard are most generally accepted. Credit and debit cards are also useful for obtaining cash from ATMS – cash machines – which are to be found in all towns and resorts. They offer the most

Where's the nearest bank/ currency exchange office?
  ¿Dónde está el banco más cercano/la oficina de cambio más cercana?
I want to change some dollars/pounds. **Quiero cambiar dólares/Libres esterlinas.**
Do you accept travellers checks? **¿Acepta usted cheques de viajero?**
Can I pay with this credit card? **¿Puedo pagar con esta tarjeta de crédito?**

convenient way of obtaining cash and will usually give you the best exchange rate.

Travellers cheques. Many hotels, larger shops, restaurants and travel agencies cash travellers cheques, and so do banks, where you're likely to get a better rate (you will need your passport). It is safest to cash small amounts at a time, thereby keeping some of your holiday funds in cheques, in the hotel safe.

O

OPENING TIMES

Shops and offices and other businesses generally observe the afternoon siesta, opening Monday–Saturday 10am–1.30pm, 5–8.30pm (some on Saturday morning only), but in tourist areas many places stay open all day, sometimes until quite late in the evening. Banks are usually open Mon–Fri, 8.30am–2pm (some open on Sat), post offices Mon–Sat 8.30am–2pm. Opening times for major museums and attractions are given in the Where to Go section of this guide.

P

POLICE

There are three police forces in the Canary Islands, as in the rest of Spain. The best known is the green-uniformed *Guardia Civil* (Civil Guard). Each town also has its own *Policía Municipal* (Municipal Police), whose uniform varies depending on the town and season, but is mostly blue and grey. The third force, the *Cuerpo Nacional de Policía*, a national anti-crime unit, can be recognised by its light brown uniform. All police officers are armed. Spanish police are strict but courteous to foreign visitors.

National police: 091
Municipal police: 092
Guardia Civil: 062

Where is the nearest police station? **¿Dónde está la comisaría más cercana?**

POST OFFICES

These are for mail, not telephone calls. Stamps (*sellos* or *timbres*) are also sold at any tobacconist's (*estanco/tabacos*) and by most shops selling postcards. Check www.correos.es for further details.

Mailboxes are painted yellow. If one of the slots is marked *extranjero*, it is for letters abroad.

Where is the (nearest) post office? **¿Dónde está la oficina de correos (más cercana)?**
A stamp for this letter/postcard, please. **Por favor, un sello para esta carta/tarjeta.**

PUBLIC HOLIDAYS

In addition to the public holidays below, many local holidays are celebrated in various towns of the archipelago (see page 99).

1 January *Año Nuevo* New Year's Day
6 January *Epifanía* Epiphany
19 March *San José* St Joseph's Day
1 May *Día del Trabajo* Labour Day
30 May *Día de las Islas Canarias* Canary Islands Day
May/June *Corpus Christi* Corpus Christi
25 July *Santiago Apóstol* St James's Day
15 August *Asunción* Assumption
12 October *Día de la Hispanidad* Discovery of America Day (Columbus Day)
1 November *Todos los Santos* All Saints' Day
8 December *Inmaculada Concepción* Immaculate Conception
25 December *Navidad* Christmas Day

T

TELEPHONES

In addition to the telephone office, Telefonica, www.telefonica.es, major towns and cities have phone booths dotted everywhere for local and international calls. Instructions in English and area codes for different countries are displayed in the booths. International calls are expensive, so be sure to have a plentiful supply of coins. Some phones accept credit cards and many require a phone card (*tarjeta telefónica*), available from tobacconists and street kiosks. For international calls, wait for the dial tone, then dial 00, wait for a second tone and dial the country code, area code (minus the initial zero) and number.

Calling directly from your hotel room is usually prohibitively expensive unless you are using a calling card, or some other similar system, from a local long distance supplier, eg AT&T or MCI. Find out from the supplier the free connection number applicable to the countries you are travelling to before you leave (they are different for each country), as these numbers are not always easily available once there.

A more convenient and economical option, but one that is only readily available in the large cities and resorts, are private companies that have a number of booths (*kioskos*) in stores, malls and other public places. These are usually highly competitive rates and you pay at the completion of the call.

The number for the International Operator is 025.

The country code for the UK is 44; US and Canada 1; Australia 61; New Zealand 64; the Republic of Ireland 353 and South Africa 27.

The telephone code for the Province of Santa Cruz de Tenerife, which includes Tenerife, El Hierro, La Gomera and La Palma is 922; for the province of Las Palmas de Gran Canaria, which includes Gran Canaria, Lanzarote and Fuerteventura, the code is 928. Don't forget that these codes must always be dialled as part of the number, even when making a local call.

TIME ZONES

In winter the Canaries use Greenwich Mean Time (GMT), which is one hour behind most European countries, including Spain, but the same as the UK. For the rest of the year the islands go on summer time, as does Spain – keeping the one-hour difference.

Winter time chart

Los Angeles	New York	London	Canaries	Madrid
4am	7am	noon	noon	1pm

TIPPING

A service charge is often included in restaurant bills, in which case a tip is not expected. If not, then add 10 percent, as you should for taxi drivers and hairdressers. In bars, customers usually leave a few coins, rounding up the bill. A hotel porter will appreciate €1 for carrying heavy bags to your room; tip hotel maids according to your length of stay.

TOILETS

The most commonly used expressions for toilets in the Canaries are *servicios* or *aseos*, though you may also hear or see WC and *retretes*. Public conveniences are rare, but most hotels, bars and restaurants have toilets. It is considered polite to buy a coffee if you do drop into a bar to use the toilet. Some café owners don't ask questions of casual visitors; other proprietors keep the key behind the bar to make sure their toilets are not used by the general public.

TOURIST INFORMATION

Information on the Canary Islands may be obtained from www.spain.info or from Spanish National Tourist Offices, which include:
Australia: International House, Suite 44, 104 Bathurst Street, PO Box A-675, 2000 Sydney NSW, tel: 02-264 7966.
Canada: 2 Bloor Street West, Suite 3402, Toronto, Ontario M4W

3E2, Canada, tel: 1416/9613131-1416/9614079.

UK: 6th floor, 64 North Row, London W1K 7DE, tel: 020 4675515/
13/16, www.tourspain.co.uk, (no personal callers at office).

US: 60 East 42nd Street, Suite 5300 (53rd Floor), New York, NY
10165-0039; Water Tower Place, suite 915 East 845, North Michigan
Ave., Chicago, ILL. 60-611; 8383 Wilshire Blvd., Suite 960, Beverly
Hills, Los Angeles, Cal.90211

For information when you are in the Canary Islands contact a
local tourist office. Most of them have staff who speak English and
German. They are mainly open Mon–Fri 10am and 2pm and 4.30–
7.30 pm Sat 10am–2pm.

Tenerife
Santa Cruz de Tenerife: Cabildo Insular, Plaza de España, tel: 922
239 592. Can supply information on the whole island.
Airport (Tenerife Sur Reina Sofia): tel: 922 392 037.
Playa de Las Américas: Centro Comercial City Centre, tel: 922
797 668.
Playa de Las Vistas: Playa de las Vistas (next to Paseo Peatonal), tel:
922 75 06 69.
El Medano: Plaza de los Principes de España, tel: 922 176 002.
La Laguna: Plaza del Adelantado, tel: 922 63 11 94.
La Oratova: Calle Carrera del Escultor Estevez 2, tel: 922 323 041.
Los Cristianos: Centro Cultural, Calle de los Playeros (opposite
petrol station), tel: 922 757 137.
Puerto de La Cruz: Plaza de Europa, tel: 922 386 000.
Santiago del Teide: Centro Comercial Seguro el Sol, Calle Manuel
Ravelo 20, tel/fax: 922 860 348.
El Hierro
Valverde: Calle Dr Quintero 4, tel: 922 550 302.
La Gomera
San Sebastián: Calle Real, 32 (Casa Bencomo), tel: 922 141 512.
Playa de Santiago: Avda. Marítima, s/n, 38812 Playa de Santiago
(Alajeró), tel: 922 895 650.

Valle Gran Rey: Calle La Noria, 2 La Playa, 38870 Valle Gran Rey, tel/fax: 922 805 458.

La Palma

Santa Cruz de La Palma: C/O'Daly,8; tel: 922 181 354.

Santa Cruz de la Palma: Avda. Blas Pérez González (opposite Post Office), tel: 922 412 106.

Gran Canaria

Las Palmas: Patronato de Turismo, calle Triana 93, tel: 928 219 600; Parque San Telmo, Calle Rafael Cabrera s/n, tel: 928 446 824; Pueblo Canario, Plaza de las Palmeras 3, tel: 928 243 593.

Airport: tel: 928 574 117.

Agüimes: Plaza de San Anton s/n, tel: 928 124 183.

San Agustin: Centro Comercial El Portón Local 11 , tel: 928 769 262.

Playa del Inglés: Avda de España/Avda eeuu, tel: 928 771 550.

Puerto de Mogán/Puerto Rico: Avda de Mogán, Local 329, tel: 928 158 804.

Teror: Plaza de Sintes , tel: 928 613 808.

Lanzarote

Arrecife: Parque José Ramírez Cerdá s/n, tel: 928 813 174.

Airport: tel: 928 820 704.

Puerto del Carmen: Avda de las Playas s/n, tel: 928 513 351.

Playa Blanca/Yaiza: El Varadero 3, tel: 928 518 150.

Fuerteventura

Puerto del Rosario: Avenida Reyes de España s/n, tel: 928 850 110.

Airport: tel: 928 860 604.

Corralejo: Avenida Marítima 2, tel: 928 866 235.

TRANSPORT (See also Getting There)

There are no train services on the islands, but the buses, on the whole, are excellent, being regular, fast and cheap.

Buses

Tenerife. Buses (*guaguas*) are operated by Transportes Interurbanos de Tenerife, SA (TITSA), tel: 922 531 300 (for 24-hour information in Spanish or English), www.titsa.com. The green buses run all over the island with surprising frequency, especially to the resorts in the south of the island. A *bono guagua* (pronounced *bono wawa*) is a multi-trip ticket that offers substantial discounts; it can be bought at the bus stations. Details of the new *tram service* between Santa Cruz and La Laguna can be found at www.tranviatenerife.com, including timetables and maps and routes.

La Gomera. Buses are operated by Guaguagomera, tel: 922 141 101; http://guaguagomera.com. They run out of San Sebastián to the main towns and tourist resorts as well as to airport several times a day in both directions.

La Palma. Buses are operated by Transportes Insular, tel: 922 411 924/922 414 441, www.transporteslapalma.com. Routes run from Santa Cruz to the airport and to Los Llanos de Aridane. The latter runs from coast to coast and passes the Visitors' Centre of the Caldera de Taburiente National Park.

El Hierro. Buses go from Valverde to main centres but are infrequent and should not be relied on for getting around the island.

Gran Canaria. In Las Palmas, buses leave from the Parque San Telmo station and the Parque Santa Catalina terminal. They are run by Global, tel: 928 252 630, www.globalsu.net. Buses to Maspalomas and Playa del Inglés are frequent and direct, and usually leave the bus terminals as soon as they are full.

Tickets on city *guaguas* cost around €1.40. A *bono guagua*, a 10-journey ticket, is good value and can be bought in terminals and kiosks. Buses run from dawn until about 10.00pm, with a night service on major routes. *Tarjetas Insulares* are good-value multi-trip tickets for trips around the island. Playa del Inglés and Maspalomas services are efficent and run to all the main out-of-town attractions.

Lanzarote. Buses run from Arrecife to Costa Teguise, Puerto del Carmen and Playa Honda every 20 minutes. Lanzarote Bus, tel: 928 811 522; http://intercitybuslanzarote.es.

Fuerteventura. Buses are operated by TIADHE (tel: 928 855 726, www.

tiadhe.com), who have services between the most important towns. However, for all north–south trips you must change in Puerto del Rosario.

Taxis

The letters SP *(servicio público)* on the front and rear bumpers of a car indicate that it is a taxi. It may also have a green light on the windscreen or a green sign indicating *'libre'* when it is available. Taxis are unmetered in tourist areas. There are fixed prices displayed on a board at the main taxi ranks, giving the fares to the most popular destinations. These are usually reasonable. If in doubt, ask the driver before you set off.

TRAVELLERS WITH DISABILITIES

There are wheelchair ramps at the major airports and many larger apartments and hotels make provision for guests with disabilities. The facilities at Los Cristianos, Tenerife, are renowned among disabled travellers. For more general information, consult the online magazine *Disability View*, Craven Publishing, 15–39 Durham Street, Kinning Park, Glasgow GW1 1BS, tel: 0141 419 0044, www.disabilityview.co.uk.

W

WEBSITES

In addition to the websites mentioned elsewhere in this book, the following are useful sources of information:
www.turismodecanarias.com: general site
www.canary-islands.com: general site and rural tourism
www.webtenerife.com: Tenerife official tourist site
www.museosdetenerife.org: Tenerife museums official site
http://elhierro.travel: El Hierro tourist site
www.museoslagomera.es: La Gomera museums site
www.grancanaria.com: Gran Canaria official tourist site
www.visitlapalma.es: La Palma tourist site
www.artesaniaymuseosdefuerteventura.org: Fuerteventura museums site
www.parquesnacionalesdecanarias.es: National Parks official site

Recommended Hotels

Accommodation in the major resorts is mostly in large, modern hotels. A lot of it is block booked by tour companies but there are usually rooms available for independent travellers, although there is little budget-price accommodation. In the towns you will find smaller hotels with more character and in rural areas there are numerous *casas rurales* (see page 116). Book well in advance, particularly during the high season (late November to March, July and August). The following is an approximate guide to prices for a double room for a night in high season (hotels are listed alphabetically within islands, not within towns):

€€€€	over 180 euros
€€€	120–180 euros
€€	60–120
€	below 60 euros

TENERIFE

Aguere €€ *Calle Rey Redondo 55, La Laguna, tel: 922 314 036*, www.hotelaguere.es. This mansion in the middle of the World Heritage quarter of town was once home to the bishop of Tenerife. The 23 recently renovated bedrooms have a simple décor and beautiful wooden floors. There is a glass-roofed café in the inner courtyard.

Botánico and Oriental Spa Garden €€€€ *Avda Richard J. Yeoward, 1, Puerto de la Cruz, tel: 922 381 400*, www.hotelbotanico.com. Set in 2.5 hectares (6 acres) of gardens and parklands, this luxury hotel has an elegant and peaceful atmosphere with views over the ocean and Mount Teide. 251 rooms.

Gran Tacande €€€ *Calle Walter Paetzman s/n, Playa de las Américas, tel: 922 970 970*, www.dreamplacehotels.com. Part of the Dreamplace resort chain found in various Canarian architectural styles. This one is by the sea with a heated salt-water pool and views over to La Gomera. Three restaurants. 248 rooms.

Horizonte € *Calle Santa Rosa de Lima 11, Puerto de la Cruz, tel: 922 271 936,* www.hotelhorizontetenerife.es. Completely refurbished in 2012, this basic hotel is conveniently situated in the city centre, but on a quiet street. 46 rooms. The parking place is charged separately.

Mare Nostrum Resort €€€€ *Avda de las Américas s/n, Playa de las Américas, tel: 936 006 545,958* www.expogrupo.com. Mega-resort comprising of three five-star hotels – Sir Anthony, Cleopatra, and Mediterranean Palace (with rooftop nudist zone and pool). Good value out of high season.

Marquesa €€ *Quintana 11, Puerto de la Cruz, tel: 922 383 151,* www. hotelmarquesa.com. One of the most beautiful mansions in town, dating from 1712; some rooms have balconies and sea views. There is a swimming pool and sauna. 150 rooms.

Parador de Cañadas del Teide €€€ *La Orotava, tel: 922 386 415,* www.paradores.es. In a stunning setting directly under El Teide, close to the cable car. Decorated in Canarian style. Pool, sauna and gym.

Rural El Patio €€€ *Finca Malpais, El Guincho, tel: 922 133 280,* www.hotelpatio.com. Inland and just east of Garachico, this rustic hotel is set in a 16th-century house on a banana plantation. A second building, Patio II, is where the plantation workers use to live. Heated pool, tennis court, croquet lawn, golf practice course, sauna and restaurant.

San Roque €€€€ *Calle Esteban de Ponte 32, tel: 922 133 435,* www. hotelsanroque.com. One of the most stylish places to stay on the island, this 18th-century mansion in the centre of Garachico has individually furnished rooms decorated with works by contemporary local artists. A large sculpture fountain by Miquel Navarro is in the main courtyard.

Sheraton Mencey €€€€ *José Navéiras 38, tel: 922 609 900,* www. grandhotelmencey.com. Old-fashioned luxury in the heart of town, close to the parliament, and used by government officials and visiting dignitaries. Tennis courts, casino, swimming pool and a top-notch restaurant. Cooking classes for children and adults.

Spring Arona Gran Hotel €€ *Avenida Juan Carlos I 38, tel: 922 750 678, www.springhoteles.com.* On a slightly scrubby stretch of beach at the end of Los Cristianos harbour, all rooms are modern and with a terrace overlooking the water. Sports facilities, restaurants, bars and a wonderful atrium lobby bedecked with green plants hanging from each floor. 400 rooms and a spa.

Tigaiga €€€ *Parque Taoro 28, Puerto de la Cruz, tel: 922 383 500, www.tigaiga.com.* Set in a lovely garden this hotel has 76 spacious rooms with full-length windows and seven junior suites overlooking Orotava Valley. Excellent restaurant.

VillAlba Spa €€ *Carretera San Roque s/n, tel: 922 709 930, www.hotelvillalba.com.* Claims to be 'the highest hotel in Spain' at 1,660m (5,450ft) above sea level. Spacious rooms with all facilities including gym. Various outdoor activities are available to book at reception.

EL HIERRO

Balneario Pozo de la Salud €€€ *Pozo de la Salud s/n, Sabinosa, tel: 922 559 561.* An elegant spa hotel offering a full range of health and beauty treatments.

Parador El Hierro €€€ *Las Playas, tel: 922 558 036, www.paradores.es.* An attractive *parador* in an isolated spot on the beach; nice pool surrounded by mountains and a restaurant serving local cuisine with a modern twist.

LA GOMERA

Gran Rey €€ *Avda. Marítima, 1, Valle Gran Rey, tel: 922 805 859, www.hotel-granrey.com.* Across from the beach and facing the fishing port this is the only hotel of note in this part of La Gomera. Rooftop pool and delightful rooms.

Jardín Tecina €€€ *Lomada de Tecina, Playa de Santiago, tel: 922 245 101, www.jardin-tecina.com.* A stylish complex set in extensive gardens on the cliffs. Friendly atmosphere combined with peaceful surroundings makes it a fantastic hideaway. An 18-hole Tecina golf course offers splendid views over the sea.

Parador Conde de la Gomera €€€ *San Sebastián de La Gomera, tel: 928 871 100*, www.paradores.es. A beautifully furnished country manor on a clifftop overlooking San Sebastián with views over to Tenerife.

LA PALMA

La Palma Romántica €€ *Crta General, Barlovento, tel: 922 186 221,* www.hotellapalmaromantica.com. Modern building in traditional style with beautiful views. Pleasant rooms, restaurant, *bodega*, spa, outdoor and indoor pool. 40 rooms.

Parador de la Palma €€€ *El Zumacal, Breña Baja, tel: 922 435 828,* www.paradores.es. A *parador* on the cliffs overlooking Santa Cruz. The décor is traditional Canarian with a delightful central patio, and it also has pleasant gardens and a pool.

Sol La Palma €€ *Playa de Puerto Naos, Los Llanos de Aridane, tel: 922 408 000,* www.solmelia.com. A modern beach-side hotel, and one of the few of any size on the west coast of the island. Restaurants, bars and swimming pools. Most of the 308 rooms have a sea view.

GRAN CANARIA

Casa de los Camellos €€, *Calle Progreso 12, Agüimes, tel: 928 785 003,* www.hecansa.com. An attractive *turismo rural* hotel in the centre of this small town, built around a shady courtyard. 12 en-suite rooms, traditionally furnished. There is a good restaurant and bar.

Christina Las Palmas €€€–€€€€ *Calle Gomera 6, Las Palmas, tel: 933 636 363* www.hotelcristinalaspalmas.com. The largest hotel in town, with 312 smart rooms. Set on the beach, it has all the extras to be expected from a five-star establishment.

IFA Buenaventura €€ *Calle Cánigo 6, Playa del Inglés, tel: 928 761 650,* www.lopesan.com. Large apartment complex – all with balconies – about 10 minutes' walk from centre. Two heated pools and Jacuzzis; six restaurants; entertainment indoors and out; karaoke; gym; four floodlit tennis courts; scuba diving school. A shopping and leisure centre is just 300m (yards) away.

Finca Las Longueras €€ *35480 Agaete, tel: 928 898 145, www. laslongueras.com.* This 19th-century mansion off the main road between Agaete and Los Barrazales has been converted into a beautiful *casa rural*. Ten carefully furnished en-suite rooms, a small pool and good Canarian food. There is also a new unit with junior suites.

La Hacienda de Buen Suceso €€€ *Carretera Arucas–Bañaderos Km 1, Arucas, tel: 928 622 945, www.haciendabuensuceso.com.* Come and be cosseted in this rural hotel set in a banana plantation just outside town. Loungey sofas on shady balconies, pool, steam room and Jacuzzi; pleasant restaurant.

Madrid € *Plazoleta de Cairasco 4, Las Palmas, tel: 928 360 664, http:// elhotelmadrid.com.* In a pretty little square in Triana, the Madrid has a long history and bags of atmosphere, which more than compensate for the somewhat old-fashioned facilities. A nice café offers daily set menus.

Puerto de Mogán €€ *Urb. Puerto de Mogán, tel: 928 565 066, www. hotelpuertodemogan.com.* A pretty little hotel right on the quayside. Friendly atmosphere, lots of personal touches, a small pool and a pleasant restaurant. The hotel also has some attractive apartments dotted around the harbour to rent.

El Refugio €€ *Cruz de Tejeda s/n, tel: 928 666 513, www.hotelruralel-refugio.com.* A wonderful place to relax after walking in the Roque Nublo Park, with a pool and sauna. 11 comfortable rooms in the hotel, 9 in the Casa Abuhardillada. Good restaurant.

Riu Grand Palace Oasis €€€€ *Plaza de las Palmeras, tel: 928 141 448, www.riu.com.* One of the most luxurious hotels on the island, set in a palm grove just a few metres/yards from the dunes.

Santa Catalina €€€€ *Parque Doramas, Calle León y Castillo 227, Las Palmas, tel: 928 243 040,* www.hotelsantacatalina.com. Set in a lush park and founded in 1890, this is the oldest, grandest and most expensive hotel in the city.

LANZAROTE

La Casona de Yaiza €€ *Calle El Rincón 11, Yaiza, tel: 928 836 262,* www.casonadeyaiza.com. This hotel in an old mansion is charming rural retreat situated near the Timanfaya National Park and Venauso Valley. Pool and good buffet breakfast. The restaurant has a great atmosphere.

Gran Meliá Salinas €€€€ *Avda Islas Canarias, s/n, Costa Teguise, tel: 928 590 040,* www.solmelia.com. The island's largest and most luxurious hotel, right on the beach. A stunning double atrium with magnificent greenery and waterfalls inspired, as is the pool, by the artist César Manrique. 289 rooms.

Los Fariones €€€ *Roque del Este, Puerto del Carmen, tel: 928 510 175,* www.farioneshotels.com. A long-established hotel on a fine beach with landscaped gardens and a large pool. Central location and excellent service. Sports centre just 90m (100yds) away.

FUERTEVENTURA

Fuerteventura Playa Blanca €€ *Playa Blanca, tel: 928 851 150.* This former *parador* stands alone, right on the beach between the capital and the airport. In a distinctive, if not beautiful building, it offers good service and ocean views.

Rural Mahoh €–€€ *Sitio Juan Bello, Villaverde, La Olivia, tel: 928 868 050,* www.mahoh.com. Early 19th-century house built of volcanic stone, with gardens, pool and multi-purpose sports pitch. Nine bedrooms furnished in traditional style.

Sol Gorriones Hotel Pájara €€€ *Playa Barca, Pájara, tel: 928 547 025,* www.solmelia.com. This large, modern hotel enjoys an isolated location beside one of the best beaches on the island; an ideal beach getaway.

INDEX

Berlitz pocket guide

Canary Islands

Eleventh Edition 2015

Written by Norman Renouf, Joby Williams
Updated by Maciek Zgliniski
Edited by Carine Tracanelli
Cartography updated by Carte
Update Production: AM Services
Picture Editor: Tom Smyth
Production: Rebeka Davies and Aga Bylica

Printed in China by CTPS

Berlitz Trademark Reg. U.S. Patent Office and other countries. Marca Registrada. Used under licence from the Berlitz Investment Corporation